What Really Matters in Writing

What Really Matters in Writing

Research-Based Practices across the Elementary Curriculum

Patricia M. Cunningham

Wake Forest University

James W. Cunningham

*Emeritus, University of North Carolina
at Chapel Hill*

ALLYN & BACON

Boston • New York • San Francisco
Mexico City • Montreal • Toronto • London • Madrid • Munich • Paris
Hong Kong • Singapore • Tokyo • Cape Town • Sydney

Executive Editor: Aurora Martínez Ramos
Series Editorial Assistant: Jacqueline Gillen
Executive Marketing Manager: Krista Clark
Marketing Manager: Danae April
Production Editor: Annette Joseph
Editorial Production Service: Lynda Griffiths
Composition Buyer: Linda Cox
Manufacturing Buyer: Megan Cochran
Electronic Composition: Denise Hoffman
Interior Design: Denise Hoffman
Cover Administrator: Linda Knowles

For related titles and support materials, visit our online catalog at www.pearsonhighered.com.

Between the time website information is gathered and then published, it is not unusual for some sites to have closed. Also, the transcription of URLs can result in typographical errors. The publisher would appreciate notification where these errors occur so that they may be corrected in subsequent editions.

Printed in the United States of America

10   9   8   7   6   5   4   HAM   13

Allyn & Bacon
is an imprint of
PEARSON

www.pearsonhighered.com

ISBN-10: 0-205-62742-0
ISBN-13: 978-0-205-62742-4

Contents

Preface

Every teacher knows that teaching students to write well is one of the most important goals we have in our elementary curriculum. Writing, however, is complex, and many teachers are unsure about which approach to take in teaching writing. Should we give students topics or let them do what real writers do and come up with their own topics? How much emphasis should we place on spelling and mechanics? What should we correct and will our corrections stifle our fledgling writers' creativity? Our goal in writing this book is to help you develop your competence and confidence in teaching writing. We will help you make and implement smart decisions about

- What to teach when
- How much structure to provide
- The level of "perfection" you should expect from your writers
- What to do about spelling
- When and how much editing and revising your students should do

and countless other issues. We will lay out a plan for teaching writing across the school year and in all areas of the elementary curriculum. Early in the school year, the plan for writing instruction will focus on students seeing writing as a way to "tell" and share their experiences and their ideas. Once students are writing willingly—if not well—you will lead them to gradually improve the quality of their writing by teaching some straightforward editing and revising strategies. By the end of the year, at any grade level, your students will demonstrate progress in the quantity and quality of their writing and will be able to do many different types of writing. You will have high expectations of your students as writers. But you will increase your demands for quality writing so gradually that your students will not be overwhelmed by the complexity of the task and lose confidence in their ability to write.

The focus of Chapter 1 is on getting students off to a successful start in writing from the first day of school. This chapter describes mini-lessons and procedures that will help your students develop confidence in themselves as writers. In

Chapter 2, you will find suggestions for early-in-the-year mini-lessons on topic selection, planning, adding on, and sharing. Because spelling is often a huge issue for teachers and a stumbling block for many students, Chapter 3 focuses on providing spelling support in your classroom so your students are free to write what they want to "tell" and not just what they can "spell." In the fourth chapter, you will find a variety of think-writes you can use as you teach math, science, social studies, and literature. Writing in all these curriculum areas will help your students learn the content of these subjects and will greatly increase the quantity of writing they do each week. Increasing the amount your students write is important because lots of writing increases the fluency and automaticity with which students write.

Chapter 5 focuses on editing. Prior to Chapter 5, the priority has been on getting your students to write willingly. Once most students are writing willingly (without much moaning and groaning), you can teach them to improve the quality of their writing by teaching them how to edit their own writing and get editing help from their friends. Chapter 6 reexamines writing across the curriculum and includes some writing activities you can use to help your students transfer their editing skills to their subject area writing. Once students have some basic editing skills, they are ready to learn to revise. Just as students can learn to edit when the editing steps are small and gradual, they can learn to revise if we break revising down into manageable steps. Your students will learn how to revise as you teach the mini-lessons described in Chapter 7. Through the activities in Chapter 8, your students will learn how to do many different types of writing in all areas of the curriculum and how to use writing scales to evaluate and revise their writing. Chapter 9 describes a variety of procedures for students to share and publish their writing.

The procedures outlined in these first nine chapters will be successful in turning most students into more able and confident writers. In every classroom, however, there are students who have particular difficulties with writing. Chapter 10 presents writing interventions you can use to help students with a variety of writing disabilities. Chapter 11 briefly summarizes the relevant research that supports the writing instruction outlined in this book.

Thank you to the following reviewers for their comments and suggestions: Kathryn A. Egawa, Seattle Public Schools, Seattle, WA; Jodi Grubb, Pittsfield Elementary School, Farmington, NH; Dena Harrison, Mendive Middle School, Sparks, NV; Madelaine Kingsbury, Overbrook High School, Philadelphia, PA; and Darlene Stewart, Pittsfield Elementary School, Belmont, NH.

The **What Really Matters** *Series*

The past decade or so has seen a dramatic increase in the interest in what the research says about reading instruction. Much of this interest was stimulated by several recent federal education programs: the Reading Excellence Act of 1998, the No Child Left Behind Act of 2001, and the Individuals with Disabilities Education Act of 2004. The commonality shared by these federal laws is that each law restricts the use of federal funds to instructional services and support that have been found to be effective through "scientific research."

In this new series we bring you the best research-based instructional advice available. In addition, we have cut through the research jargon and at least some of the messiness and provide plain-language guides for teaching students to read and write. Our focus is helping you use the research as you plan and deliver instruction to your students. Our goal is that your lessons be as effective as we know how, given the research that has been published.

Our aim is that all children become active and engaged readers and writers and that all develop the proficiencies needed to be strong independent readers and writers. Each of the short books in this series features what we know about one aspect of teaching and learning to read and write independently. Each of these pieces is important to this goal but none is more important than the ultimate goal: active, strong, independent readers and writers who read and write eagerly

So, enjoy these books and teach your students all to read and write.

Chapter 1

Getting Writing Off to a Good Start

Successful teaching of any subject requires a proper mix of idealism and realism.

If you were like we were during our first year of teaching, you began by being overly idealistic and ended by being overly realistic, with a commitment to maintain more of a balance next year! Such a balance is especially important when teaching writing. Yes, writing presents us with special challenges. For example, many students come to us less motivated to write than they are to read. That is understandable (we're being realists here!) because children are less likely to witness writing for pleasure or to achieve goals at home than they are to witness reading for those purposes. For another example, writing development is not as well understood by administrators or the public as reading and math development are. So, while no one expects first-graders to do long division of numbers with decimals or fifth-graders to read and interpret Shakespeare, people often criticize pieces of elementary writing because they contain errors on rules not taught until middle or high school.

Yet, these challenges and others cannot diminish the importance of children learning to write well in today's society or the satisfaction that elementary teachers and their students gain when a good writing program has been established in their classrooms. To help you meet these challenges and experience this satisfaction, we have strived to attain a suitable mix of idealism and realism in this book. In fact, we don't see idealism and realism as opponents, but as friends. Only by acknowledging the real difficulties that can arise when teaching writing to a broad range of students can we help all our students to reach lofty goals.

Like all other components and aspects of effective writing instruction, getting all students off to a good start in writing must not be taken for granted (too idealistic!) or considered impossible (too realistic!), but is achieved when we anticipate problems and meet them with sensible solutions.

Getting Students to Write

"Some of my students refuse to write. How do you get everyone to be willing to write?"

"If I let them choose what to write about, many of my students won't write."

"When I let them choose, they just write the same thing over and over."

"My class won't write if I don't spell for them!"

Could you hear your voice in any of these statements? Are you sometimes frustrated by your students' unwillingness to cooperate in the kind of writing instruction you know is best for them? As you start the year with a new class, your students may be wary of how you will respond to their writing. They know their writing is not perfect. There are always words they are unsure about how to spell and mechanical rules and conventions they forget or misuse. To get your students off to a successful start in writing, you must show them that the thing you care most about in their writing is that they write what they want to tell and tell it in as interesting and genuine way as they can. You can do this by modeling in your own writing something you want to tell them and then responding enthusiastically to whatever they tell you in their writing. We call this beginning phase of writing *self-selected writing* because students come up with their own topics for writing.

All children have personal lives—lives they live outside of school—mornings, evenings, weekends, school holidays, and vacations from school. By teaching your students that they can write about what they already know, you help them overcome the lack of knowledge they may have about any topic that might be suggested or assigned to them. By teaching children that they can write about what they already care about, you help them overcome the lack of interest they may have in writing about a topic they don't care about. When children refuse to write because you don't give them a topic, they are showing you that they consider writing to be something kids do in school but that has no relationship to their real lives. You can use self-selected writing to gradually change your students' attitudes that writing is a school-based rather than a personal activity.

At the beginning of each year, we don't take students through the writing process. We only have them do a first draft. If you teach older children, you may not see the need for this if many of your students write well and willingly. But, every class has some students who lack self-confidence or intrinsic motivation to write and refuse to write or write only the bare minimum. Students who have not learned to value writing or who avoid writing out of fear of failure or imperfection are likely to fail if they are expected to revise, edit, or recopy a piece of writing before their intrinsic motivation, self-confidence, or independence in writing significantly improve. Single-draft writing on self-selected topics for several days or weeks can get ALL your students off to a successful start, regardless of what grade they are in.

What About My Advanced Writers?

Your advanced writers will shine. They already write well and willingly and they will enjoy the freedom to choose their topics and "strut their stuff!" Your unwilling writers are the reason you need to start with single-draft writing on self-selected topics, but your wonderful writers will enjoy and profit from this kid-centered beginning. Remember this is only how you get the year off to a successful start. By the end of the year, your writing instruction will be much more sophisticated.

Writing the First Week of School

To get your writing year off to a successful start, the first time you ask your students to write is very important. It will send a message about you—and writing—and how you view writing. Your first writing sessions will anchor your students' sense of themselves as writers in your classroom. Use these first writing lessons to demonstrate what you most value in their writing. For your mini-lessons, write something about your life that you think will interest your students. After they watch you write, give them a brief time—no more than 10 minutes for the first several writing sessions—to write something about their lives they are willing to share with the class. Tell them that you will let volunteers share what they have written but that no one will be required to share. The very first words out of your mouth about writing might sound something like this, depending on what grade you teach:

> Boys and girls, we are off to a good start on our first day of school. We have reviewed some of our rusty math facts and shared some of our favorite books. Now we are going to get to know each other better by sharing some things we care about in our lives. I'm going to share with you some things that are important in my life and then I want you to share with me and the class some important things in your life. Instead of telling you, I'm going to write what I want to share. You are welcome to read aloud what I am writing and you can even guess what words I will use before I write them if you think you know.

Now, write something—as your students watch. Do not read aloud what you are writing but encourage your students to read it aloud—and predict from the context and a few letters what word you are writing. Because so many words are easily predicted based on first letters and syntax, your students will often correctly anticipate the word you are about to write and they will experience a sense of satisfaction by how often they guess the correct word when just a

letter or two has been written. When you finish writing, invite the class to read your piece with you and ask questions and make comments about what you have written.

My Family

Of all the important things in my life, my family is probably most important. I met my husband in college and we have been married for ten years. He is the manager of the Top Cow Steak House in Burlington. We have two sons, Ian and Kevin. Ian is 6 and is in Mrs. Harper's class. Kevin is 3 and is in preschool at Step Ahead. Ian takes karate lessons after school and is on a soccer team. Kevin follows Ian around and wants to do everything Ian does! We have two other members of our family, Squeaky and Harriet. Squeaky is a huge black and white cat. He is very friendly and loves to be petted by anyone. Harriet is a tiny gray kitten who hides when anyone comes to the house and is afraid of everything! Someday I will bring my whole family, including Squeaky and Harriet, to school so you can meet them.

Perhaps you noticed that this first piece of teacher writing is fairly mundane—not particularly clever or humorous or remarkable. To your students, however, this is really interesting stuff! Kids love to know things about their teacher's personal life—and there are many things in the piece students will respond to. Karate and soccer are hot topics for many children as are pets of any sort. The idea of a younger sibling following you around is well known to most children! The first piece you write should not be extraordinary—but it should communicate something about yourself that your students will find interesting.

Once you and your students have read the piece aloud, give them a few minutes to ask you some questions and make comments sharing connections they have made:

"How old is Squeaky?

"Do Squeaky and Harriet play together?"

"Is Harriet afraid of Squeaky?"

"I was in Mrs. Harper's room in first grade."

"My cousin goes to Step Ahead Daycare."

"Where does Ian take karate lessons?"

Next, give the students a piece of paper or a writing notebook and tell them to write about something important in their lives. When someone asks if you want them to write about their families or pets, tell them that you would love to know more about their families or pets if that is what is important to them right now. When someone protests that she doesn't have any pets, assure that student that you will be interested in whatever she wants to share, and that everyone is not going to write about the same thing you wrote about. Give them a short time—not more than 10 minutes—to write. As they write, circulate and respond to their topics. Make your comments in a hushed but audible voice so that children can hear your encouraging comments.

"I see someone else has a little brother who follows him around."

"That's interesting. I also learned to swim in the summer before third grade."

"Ian wants to go to camp next summer. I'd love to know more about the camp you went to."

What If?

What if Some Students Don't Write Anything?

Ignore them! Walk right on past their desks and give your attention to someone who is making an effort. Resist the urge to give them a topic or otherwise take over the responsibility for their writing. When your reluctant writers see you giving your attention to those who are writing and expressing interest in their topics, some of them will begin to put down a few words. When you see them make any attempt, move to them. Marvel at their topic. Help them stretch out words. Tell them you can't wait to hear more about their fascinating topic! It is a rare reluctant writer who can persist in not writing day after day if you persist in giving your attention to those who are writing!

If the children ask you to spell a word, explain that you cannot spell words for them when they are writing a first draft because it slows everyone down.

I don't want you to worry about spelling now because no one but you is going to read this piece. Just spell it as best you can so you can remember what you want to tell if you share what you have written. Later in the year, we will publish some pieces and then I will help you fix all the spelling so that your friends and parents can easily read what you wrote.

If your reluctant speller doesn't seem able or willing to spell the word at all, you may want to help that student stretch out the word and write down the letters she hears:

What word are you trying to spell? California! That is a very tough word to spell. Do you know the first letter? Yes, California begins with a C. Put that down. Say California slowly and I bet you can hear some other letters you know. Yes, there is an a and an l and an f and an e and an n. Put down all the letters you hear or think are there and you will have enough to remember what you were writing if you choose to share this with all of us in a few minutes.

When the writing time is up, circle your students and ask who wants to share what they have been writing. After someone has shared, model how to ask a question and how to make a connection comment. Invite classmates who have questions or comments to make them.

"Where did you take swimming lessons? I want to learn to swim."

"Does your grandma like living here with you or does she miss her friends in California? I bet you like having your grandma live with you."

Don't let the sharing go on too long. Assure students who didn't get to share today that there will be other chances to share tomorrow.

Before sending your students back to their seats, draw their attention to a chart titled *Things I Might Write About* that you have displayed somewhere in the room.

I got some good ideas from your writing today that I don't want to forget, so I'm going to list a few ideas on my Things I Might Write About list.

Go to the chart and as your students watch, jot down a few ideas clearly related to what various students wrote. Suggest to your students that if they got any good writing ideas, they should write them down so they won't forget them. Give them a few minutes when they go to their seats to start their writing ideas list.

```
┌─────────────────────────────────────────────────────────────┐
│                  Things I Might Write About                   │
│   1.  Learning to Swim                                        │
│   2.  My Grandma                                              │
│   3.  My Little Sister                                        │
│   4.  Moving to a New School                                 │
│   5.  Camp                                                    │
└─────────────────────────────────────────────────────────────┘
```

Think about this first writing session. What has been accomplished? What message have you communicated to your students? Imagine that over the next week, you write several more "mundane" pieces—modeling how you are reminded of some topics you wanted to write about by pondering your *Things I Might Write About* list before you begin writing. Each day, as you write, encourage your students to read aloud and anticipate words as you are writing. After you finish writing, lead your students to chorally read what you have written and ask a few questions and make a few comments.

After they watch you write, give your students a few minutes to write. As with the earlier writing, circulate among your students, making encouraging comments in a quiet but audible voice. Again, don't spell words for them but help them stretch out words and get down some important letters if they need that assistance. Praise them for using big, vivid words they are unsure about how to spell rather than common words they can spell.

Terrified! What a wonderful word to describe how you felt when you realized you had gotten lost at the park! I bet you can spell *scared* or *afraid* but they don't come close to painting the picture that *terrified* does. You have the *t* written. Say *terrified* slowly and put down any other letters you hear or know are there. Good! You have plenty of letters to help you remember what you wrote if you share this experience with us! I hope you will. I bet many of your classmates have been lost or felt terrified. In fact, that gives me another idea to add to my own writing list.

When the writing time is up, circle your students and let volunteers share. Continue to model asking questions and making connection comments. Comment on the use of vivid words such as *terrified*. Point out to everyone that the writer could have used a common—and easily spelled—word, such as *afraid* or *scared*. Then reinforce the idea that in your classroom, you want your students to write what they want to tell—not just what they can spell! As each person shares, let that person call on a few friends to ask a question or make a comment. When the sharing time is over, add an idea or two to your writing topic ideas list and encourage your students to add to their lists.

Things I Might Write About

1. Learning to Swim
2. My Grandma
3. My Little Sister
4. Moving to a New School
5. Camp
6. Ian Getting Lost at the Mall
7. Things That I Am Terrified Of

By the end of this first week of school, you will have successfully launched your students into writing. They will know that what you value most are their ideas and that to you, writing is first and foremost about sharing ideas with others. You can now move forward and begin to include in your mini-lessons some of the writing strategies all good writers need to learn. You have accomplished the first and most important step. You have "hooked" them all on writing!

Getting Started with a Whole Class of Reluctant Writers

In most classrooms, the procedures described in the previous section will launch your students successfully into writing. Unfortunately, some classrooms are full of students who are really reluctant to write or who refuse to write. In this section, we will describe two highly structured ways of getting your kids into writing when they are determined that they can't or they won't! *The Five Steps* is appropriate for kindergarten or first grade. *Can't Stop Writing* has been successfully used with students in second grade through middle school. (If you don't have a whole class of resistant writers, skip this section and move forward with the ideas in Chapter 2.)

The Five Steps

The Five Steps is a modification of *The Four Steps* (Fisher, 1991). The steps are:

1. Think.
2. Draw a picture.
3. Write something.
4. Write your name.
5. Stamp or write the date.

The first mini-lessons in *The Five Steps* teach children what the five steps are and how to do them. Begin your mini-lesson with a blank transparency or a piece of drawing paper with no lines on it and say something like this:

> Boys and girls, in a few minutes I want you to do *The Five Steps*. So that you'll know what I want you to do, I am going to do *The Five Steps* and let you watch me. Before I do that, repeat after me what the five steps are:
>
> 1. Think. (They repeat as you raise one finger.)
> 2. Draw a picture. (They repeat as you raise another finger.)
> 3. Write something. (They repeat as you raise another finger.)
> 4. Write your name. (They repeat as you raise another finger.)
> 5. Stamp or write the date. (They repeat as you raise the fifth finger.)
>
> So, what's the first step? Yes, I need to think about what I want to draw. Have I seen anything interesting in the past few days? Have I done something interesting that I would like to tell you about? Let me think. I know. Ian got a bike for his birthday. I will draw him with his bike and the training wheels.

> Pick up a marker and begin drawing. Be sure to draw a simple and primitive picture that will not intimidate your students into thinking they must be artistic to

do this step. (Some of us who are less artistic won't have any trouble doing that!) While drawing, talk about what you are drawing.

> Here is the bike and I need to draw the training wheels here. Now I am drawing Ian on the bike. He is looking very pleased as he heads off down the street.

Don't take more than a few minutes to draw your picture. When you have finished drawing, put down your marker. Then, say something like,

> I've thought and I've drawn a picture. Now it's time for me to do the third step. I'm going to write something about my picture.

Using a black marker, print something about the picture you have drawn:

> Ian is learning to ride his new bike.

> Now it's time for me to do the fourth step. Does anyone remember the next step after we write something? Yes, it's time for me to write my name.

Write your name somewhere on the paper. For the fifth step, model for your students how you want them to write or stamp the date.

My new puppy will sleep on a baby blanket in a box like this.

Mr. Cunningham

SEP 16 2012

Next, give your students unlined paper and crayons and tell them it is their turn to do *The Five Steps*. Remind them of what you did for each step.

> What did I do first? Yes, I had to think about what I wanted to draw. Everyone take one minute and think.

After one minute, ask the students to pick up a crayon and draw what they were thinking about.

> Now it's time for you to do the second step. Pick up a crayon and draw what you are thinking. When you are finished drawing, I will give you a pencil so you can write something to go with your drawing.

From the time the thinking step begins until you end the activity should be about 10 to 15 minutes. As the children move through the five steps, circulate and encourage them. "Ooh and aah" about the interesting things they are drawing and writing about and comment that many of them are much better artists than you are. Do not spell words for them but do help them stretch out words and encourage them to use any words you have displayed in your print-rich classroom. When the time is up, circle your students and let them tell about their drawing and writing. Model questions and connection comments and praise those students who completed all five steps.

What If?

What if Some Students Draw but Don't Write Anything?

During the first few lessons, it is not unusual for some children to spend all the time working on their pictures, so that they complete only the first two steps in the time allotted. It is important not to allow extra time for these children to complete the steps but rather to encourage them to try to complete all five steps the next time. If you stick to your time limit, most children will gradually spend less time on their drawings so they have time to complete all five steps. If you have your children raise their hands when they have finished drawing and hand them a pencil, you can also give them a smile or quick word of praise for having completed their drawing. Your students will learn to monitor their drawing time by noticing that other children are finishing their drawings and moving on to writing with their pencils.

The Five Steps is a successful way to get reluctant kindergarten and first-grade children to write early in the year. It succeeds partly because young children are more willing to decide what they will draw than what they will write. Once they have drawn, they have their topic for writing. If you use the various implements, drawing crayons, writing pencils, and date stamp, children will learn to move through the five steps. You may want to post a chart to remind your children of *The Five Steps*.

Can't Stop Writing

Can't Stop Writing (also called *Sustained Silent Writing*) is a way to begin writing with students in second grade through middle school, if you have many students who are unwilling or unable to write. *Can't Stop Writing* is a "can't fail" approach to begin the year because it has only one essential rule: You can't stop writing until the timer goes off! This activity is always timed. Most teachers set the timer for three minutes to begin with and then gradually increase the time as students become more willing to write. To teach what *Can't Stop Writing* is and how it works, model it in a mini-lesson.

> In a few minutes, I want you to do *Can't Stop Writing*. So you'll know exactly what I want you to do, I'm going to do *Can't Stop Writing* and let you watch me. The first thing I have to do is to think of what I will write about. So, now I have to think about what I will write while you watch me. Have I seen anything interesting in the past few days? Have I done something interesting that I would like to write about? Let me think.

At this point, you should pause and then mention one or two things that you have done or seen lately that you might write about. Make sure they are things your students can relate to.

> I know. This weekend our whole family went to the new park. We rented canoes and paddled down the river. We hiked on lots of the trails. It is a great park and I am so glad it is finally open.

After mentioning a couple of examples like this one, decide out loud to the class which one you will write about. Then, say something like,

> I've thought about what I'm going to write about. Now it is time for me to do *Can't Stop Writing*.

Set a timer for three minutes and turn it so the students can see how much time is left, but you cannot. Begin writing and do not say aloud what you writing as you write. Your students will pay better attention if they are trying to read what you are writing as you write it. Do not write too fast or use such big words that you intimidate them with your writing proficiency. You want your students to believe they can do what you are doing. Thirty or forty seconds into your writing, without comment, begin writing,

> I can't think of anything else to write. I can't think of . . .

Then resume writing as you were before. Your students will probably titter, but you should continue on as if nothing has happened. Perhaps do this again toward the end.

When the timer goes off, unless you are at the end of a sentence, say something like this,

> The rule is I get to finish the sentence I am writing.

Then, quickly finish that sentence and read aloud to your students what you have written (crossing through the "I can't think of anything to write" sentences). If your students want to ask a question or make a comment about what you wrote, encourage them but keep it brief.

> We have a screened porch on the back of our house. I love to sit out there when the weather is warm enough and look out into our backyard. We have some trees so there are usually birds and squirrels to watch. I guess they can't see me through the screen! ~~I can't think of anything else to write. I can't think of~~ The other day, our neighbor's cat came sneaking into our yard. She loves to try to catch a bird or squirrel. You should have heard the squirrels up in the trees hissing at her. That warns the other squirrels and the birds, too! Sometimes I'm afraid the cat will catch one of them, so I yell at her to go home. It's not like she isn't well fed. In fact, she could go on a diet and it wouldn't hurt her a bit.

Next, tell your students it is time for them to do *Can't Stop Writing*. Tell them that there is only one rule: You can't stop writing until the timer goes off. Remind them of how you wrote "I can't think of anything to write" a time or two and then continued. Assure them that they can cross those sentences out at the end just as you did.

Have your students write their names and today's date at the top of their papers and put down their pencils. Then tell them they have one minute to think about what they will write about today. During this time, do not let anyone start writing. After exactly one minute, tell everyone to begin writing. Set the timer for three minutes and turn its face away so that neither you nor they can see how much time is left. Even though you wrote during your mini-lesson, you should also write again while they write. Later, you will want to circulate and encourage them by "ooing and aahing" about their topics and helping them stretch out words they need to spell, but for the first several lessons, it is probably better to stay out of their space and model writing once again.

When the timer goes off, tell the students that they are allowed to quickly finish the sentence they are writing and then they must stop. Ask for volunteers to share what they wrote by reading it aloud to the class. Remind the children that you skipped over your "I can't think of anything else to write" while sharing, because it wouldn't be interesting to hear. Ask them to skip over any "I can't think . . . " parts and just read the interesting parts.

Do *Can't Stop Writing* each day. When all your students can sustain their writing for three minutes, add a minute until your students can sustain their writing for four minutes. After that, gradually add a minute at a time until your students are able to sustain their writing for six or seven minutes. After they can sustain their writing for this amount of time, you have accomplished your goal of getting them started writing and can focus your mini-lessons on some of the activities in the following chapters.

Looking Back
Getting Writing Off to a Good Start

To launch your students successfully into writing:

- Write something your students will be interested in for your daily mini-lesson.
- Model and talk about correct writing, but don't expect it from students.
- Model how you come up with topics, but don't give them topics.
- Help the children "phonic or sound" spell and find words in the room, but don't spell words for them. (Much more about this is discussed in Chapter 3.)
- "Ooh and aah" about their topics and clever ideas.
- If you have a class full of really resistant writers, consider starting with *The Five Steps* or *Can't Stop Writing*.

Chapter 2

What Do I Do Once
I Have Them Writing?

Cheer! Breathe a sigh of relief! Celebrate!

Getting your students to the point that they are willing to write on topics they care about is the most important step in establishing a successful writing program in your classroom. Once your students are writing and sharing, you can begin to teach some mini-lessons on choosing topics, adding on, and planning. As you teach these mini-lessons, you are still teaching them by modeling what you want them to learn and then encouraging them to try the processes you have modeled in their own writing. You are still doing only first-draft writing and letting volunteers share as they feel comfortable sharing. The other steps of the writing process—revising, editing, and publishing—will be added as the year goes on and your students become more confident in themselves as writers.

Deciding What to Write About (Choosing Topics)

If you began your writing year in the way described in the previous chapter, you have already begun helping your students get over the "What do I write about?" dilemma. The most important thing you have done is to show them that writing is putting down on paper what one wants to tell. You show them this by writing about things you want to tell them and then encouraging them to write about things they want to tell you and the class.

Things I Might Write About Lists

You have also helped your students choose topics by beginning your own *Things I Might Write About* list and giving them a few minutes after the sharing time each day to add things to their lists if the writing of their classmates inspired them to write about certain topics. Continue to add to your list and cross things off as you write about them. On some days, let your students hear you use the list to decide.

> Let's see. I don't have anything particularly interesting happening in my life right now that I want to tell you about. What shall I write about? I think I will look at my list and see if I find any inspiration there.

Look over at your list and think aloud about several items on the list before settling on one.

> I could write about how I learned to swim or my grandma. I already wrote about my little sister and going to camp. I haven't told you about when I was in third grade and had to move to a new school in the middle of the year. Would you like me to write about that?

When your students respond enthusiastically, you begin to write. You don't read aloud what you are writing but you encourage your students to read as you write. The students enjoy reading what you are writing and try to predict each word based on the context and the first few letters. When you have finished writing, lead your students to chorally read what you have written and ask a few questions or make a few connection comments. Cross "Moving to a New School" off your list and then circulate, encouraging your students as they write and helping them stretch out words if they need that help.

Things I Might Write About

1. Learning to Swim
2. My Grandma
3. ~~My Little Sister~~
4. ~~Moving to a New School~~
5. ~~Camp~~
6. Ian Getting Lost at the Mall
7. Things that I Am Terrified Of
8. ~~Football~~
9. Tornadoes
10. Carving a Jack-o-Lantern

Class Lists of Things We All Know About

In addition to individual lists, you may want to create a class list of things your students know a lot about. Ask the students some questions that most of them will answer positively and then add these topics to a class list.

Raise your hand if you have brothers or sisters. Most of you do. Let's add brothers and sisters.

I like to eat pizza and ice cream. What do you like to eat? I will add some of our class's favorite foods to the list.

As the year goes on, add to the list of topics that all your students know about. If someone shares a piece of writing about a neighbor, ask your students to raise their hands if they have neighbors. Assuming almost everyone admits to having neighbors, add "Neighbors" to the class list.

When you finish a unit of study or theme, add that topic and some of the subtopics to the list.

> We have just finished learning about Magnets and Electricity. What topics can we add to the list now that everyone in our class knows a lot about?

If you have a visitor who talks about a topic your students are interested in or if the class takes a fieldtrip, add those topics to your list. Don't overwhelm your students with the number of topics on the class list, but do be on the alert to add to it when there is genuine interest on the part of your students. Here is a list of topics one group of children helped the teacher create early in the year. The students in this class never complained that they didn't know what to write about!

Things Room 22 Knows a Lot About

1. Brothers and Sisters	11. Cousins
2. TV Shows	12. Baseball
3. School	13. P.E.
4. Pizza	14. Soccer
5. McDonald's	15. Music
6. Neighbors	16. Lunch
7. Swimming	17. Dogs
8. Wal-Mart	18. Tornadoes
9. Cars and Trucks	19. Our Gerbil
10. Fall Festival	20. Butterflies

Teacher Think-aloud About Possible Topics

Another clever tactic you might use to help students decide what to write about is to think aloud about a few topics with which you know many children have had experiences.

> Let's see, what do I want to tell you about today? I could write about the new bike Ian got for his birthday and how he is learning to ride it. I could write about what happened in our room yesterday when the power went off. I could write about seeing some of you at the football game Friday night and how surprised you were to see me there. I could write about the dog I had when I was your age. That's it! That's what I want to tell you about today. I will write about Gorlab.

As you think aloud before writing about a few topics of interest to your students that you don't write about—your son's new bike, the power outage in the classroom yesterday, seeing some of the students at Friday's football game—you are planting some ideas for what your students may want to write about. Without giving the students a writing topic, clever teachers plant suggestions that help their students remember something interesting they may not have thought about as a good writing topic.

Family Help in Coming Up with Topics

Send a letter home to your students' families asking them to help their children come up with topics they know a lot about. Explain that the topics should not be "family secrets" but could include family members, traditions, places visited, other places lived, favorite activities, and so on. Limit the number of items to five so that no one feels they have to complete an exhaustive list. Keep the letter short and write the first draft of the letter for your mini-lesson so that the children get to watch you creating it. If your students are beginning readers, have them read it with you a few times so that they can impress their family with their reading skills!

Dear Family,

As you probably have heard, we write every day in our classroom. We write about what we want to tell and have written many interesting pieces already. Children write best when they are writing about things they know about and care about. Please help your child come up with some topics they know a lot about—family members, traditions, trips, favorite activities, and others. (No family secrets, please!) Thank you for your help.

Child's Name_____

Here are five topics my child knows a lot about and might want to write about:

1.

2.

3.

4.

5.

Photos to Inspire Writing

Across a week's time, take photos of your students doing various activities. Include lots of different settings in your school environment (kids getting off their buses, in the classroom, at the media center or computer lab, on the playground, in the gym, at lunch, and so on). Be sure to include yourself and other teachers and school staff in some of the photos. If you have class pets, they should also be included in the photo gallery. Refuse to divulge your reasons for taking all these photos. (Every classroom needs a certain amount of intrigue!)

When you have a good number of photos—including all your students in at least one photo, attach these to a bulletin board and number them. Do a mini-lesson in which you describe one of the photos and let the children guess which numbered photo you were writing about. Be prepared for a few weeks in which many of your students write about various photos and beg to share their writing and have their classmates guess which photo they were writing about!

George is are pet gerbil. Last week it was my turn to take care of him. I fed him gerbil food and seeds and raisins for treats. I put fresh water in his bottle. Every day I held him for 10 minutes. I pet his fur and rubed his tummy. I asked my mom for a gerbil for my birthday.

Planning

Planning what you are going to write before you start, and then planning what you will write next while you are writing is an essential skill for all writers. As soon as your students are willing to write on what they know and care about without you spelling words for them, they are ready to learn how to improve as planners of their writing. There are many different mini-lessons you can teach to help students learn how to plan or plan better. Here are some to get you started.

Turn and Talk

On some days, have your students plan what they are going to write by giving them two minutes (one minute each) to turn to a neighbor and talk about what they are going to write. Most children would much rather talk than write, so be sure to set the timer and limit each child to one minute. Talking about what they will write helps them plan, but it's important to stick to your time limits so that everyone has time to actually write.

Graphic Organizers

Graphic organizers are excellent planning devices for writers, but they must be kept simple so that the writing—not the making of the organizer—remains the main event. The easiest kind of organizer is simply a listing of ideas related to the topic. To do a mini-lesson on clustering, for example, you might choose one of the topics from your personal list and then let your students watch as you brainstorm words related to that topic. The cluster (sometimes called a *web*) for the topic "butterflies" might look like the accompanying illustration.

Writing the cluster—and thinking aloud about how you are making it—would be your mini-lesson for one day. On the next day, take your cluster out and review it before writing about butterflies. Refer to your cluster as you are writing to make sure you don't forget any important ideas. Tell your students that they may want to make a cluster of ideas before writing about some of their topics. Once you have modeled for them how you create a cluster and then use it to help you stay on track with your writing, make the cluster one day, then write using that cluster the next day. Over the next several weeks, model a few more times how you can cluster ideas to plan your writing, and remind students how they can use clusters to plan their writing.

A special type of cluster many children enjoy using is the *Five Finger Planner* (Rog, 2007). To model the use of this planner, let students watch as you trace your hand. Write the topic of your writing on the palm and then write four details you want to include—one on each of the four fingers. A conclusion or feeling you have about the topic is written on the thumb.

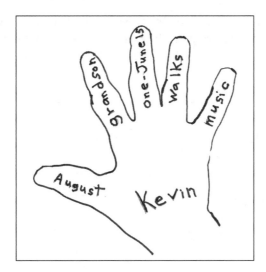

When you have finished your *Five Finger Planner*, put it aside and tell your students that tomorrow you will use this to help you remember what you want to write. For tomorrow's mini-lesson, review what you have written on the five fingers and then let your students watch you turn this into a paragraph about your topic. Add more details as you write so that students see that the plan is just the basic idea that you elaborate on as you write.

Kevin

Kevin is my grandson. He was one year old on June 15. He has just started to walk and falls down a lot! He loves music and tries to sing and dance. I can't wait to see him when we go to Rhode Island in August.

You may want to have copies of a *Five Finger Planner* template available for students to use when they want to use this device to plan their writing. Make sure students understand that they don't always need to use this device for planning but that copies are available for them if they choose to. Model this in your mini-lessons by periodically using the *Five Finger Planner* to plan one day what you write the next day.

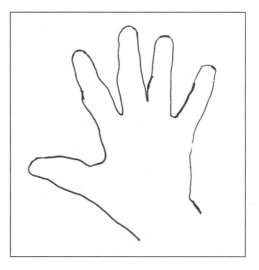

The other planning organizer you might use is a Venn diagram, or what we like to call a *Double Bubble*. Plan writing in which you compare two things by letting the students watch you create your *Double Bubble* one day and write from it the next day.

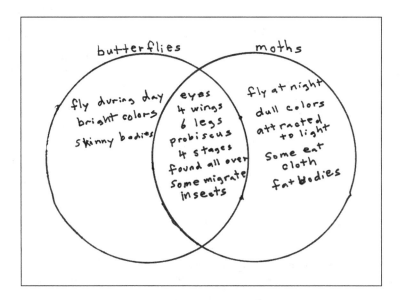

Clusters, webs, and double bubbles are the simplest planning devices, and so you can use them early in the year to help students begin planning writing. As the year continues and you begin to focus your mini-lessons on editing, revising, and publishing, you may continue to use these organizing devices and, depending on the age and sophistication of your students, introduce more complex or genre-specific graphic organizers.

Why Not?

Why Not Plan Before Writing Every Day?

Because all writers don't write in the same way! All writers plan but some plan in their heads. Many writers discover what they want to say as they are writing. Planning is a good thing to model and teach your students but don't overdo it. Show your students that there are different ways to plan—including talking with a friend—and that sometimes they can just write without an external planning step.

Moving Beyond One Sentence and Adding On

Another type of mini-lesson you may want to include early in the year focuses on writing more than one sentence and adding on to a piece begun on the previous day. You have already shown your students some ways to move beyond one sentence if you have demonstrated some planning devices such as clusters, webs, and double bubbles. Here are a few other ideas teachers have found successful.

Writing One Sentence and Saying, "I'm Done!"

This is something many children do but they are shocked when you do it! Choose a topic. Write one sentence, put your marker down, look at your children and announce, "I'm done."

> My cousin had a baby last night.

Your students are sure to have questions. Encourage and answer their questions orally but do not write them.

> "What's your cousin's name?" ("Amy.")
>
> "Where does she live?" ("In Iowa.")
>
> "Is the baby a boy or a girl?" ("A boy.")
>
> "How big is the baby?" ("8 pounds and 4 ounces.")

Let your students continue to ask questions and answer them orally. Then, with surprise in your voice, say something like,

> "Goodness. I have lots to tell you about the new addition to our family!"

Return to your piece and write some more, including as much of the information as is relevant. Do this a few more times across the next several weeks until you feel that your students understand how they can expand beyond their first sentence by thinking about questions people might ask about it.

On another day, give all your students index cards and ask them to write only one sentence about a topic they know a lot about. Collect the cards and choose a sentence to write on the overhead or chart. Here is Taylor's sentence:

My birthday is on Friday.

Encourage the children to ask Taylor questions and have Taylor answer them. Give Taylor back his card and comment that he certainly knows what his friends would like to know about his birthday plans.

Choose another card and write another sentence. Here is Chandra's sentence:

My team won the game.

Encourage the children to ask Chandra questions and again hand her back her card and comment on how much everyone would like to know. Continue to write a few more children's sentences and let others ask questions until your mini-lesson time is up. If you think more practice is needed, write a few more of your children's sentences for a second day's mini-lesson.

On another day, follow this up by again giving your students index cards and asking them to write one sentence. Have the children count off so that you have three students in each group. Let each group gather somewhere in the room and have each student read his or her sentence and let the other children ask questions.

Writing one sentence and saying, "I'm done" is an amazingly simple—and effective—device for helping your students learn to expand their writing beyond one sentence.

Who? What? When? Where? Why?

Another way to get children to expand their writing is to have other students ask these five W questions. Tell your class that these are questions that reporters often try to answer as they write newspaper stories. You may want to read them a short newspaper article or article from a children's magazine, such as *Time for Kids* or *Zoobooks,* and have them determine if the five W questions were answered. Next, title the piece with what you want to write about and have the children ask you Who? What? When? Where? and Why? questions. Give them oral answers to their questions and then use some of this information as you write your piece. Many teachers display a chart with these five W questions and also refer to it during reading comprehension lessons.

```
┌─────────────────────────────────────────┐
│                                         │
│              The 5 W Facts              │
│                                         │
│      We all want to know all the facts: │
│                                         │
│              Who?                       │
│                                         │
│              What?                      │
│                                         │
│              When?                      │
│                                         │
│              Where?                     │
│                                         │
│              Why?                       │
│                                         │
└─────────────────────────────────────────┘
```

Use the procedure described for the "I'm done" lessons to get your students involved in asking each other the five W questions.

Adding On

One of the major concepts you want to get across to your students early in the year is that writers don't always finish the piece they are working on in one day. Each day as they begin their writing time, remind the students that they can begin a new piece or add on to the piece they were working on the day before. If, in spite of your reminders, almost none of your students add on to their pieces and almost all of them begin a new topic each day, plan some mini-lessons in which you begin a piece one day but don't have time to finish. Begin writing your piece as you do each day in front of the children. When the time you have allotted to your mini-lesson is up, stop writing and remark,

> I didn't know I had so much to say about _____. I will continue this tomorrow.

Your students may protest and ask you to continue but be persistent and remind them that if you take too much time in your mini-lesson, it will cut into their writing time. The following day, pull out your piece and reread it aloud to "get back your train of thought." (You may want to have your students read it with you. There is no such thing as too much reading practice.) After you have reread, then continue writing. Depending on what you are writing about, you may finish on the second day or you may need to continue on the third day. Regardless of how many days it takes you to complete a piece, be sure to reread everything you have written to get back on track with what you have said and still want to say.

After a few adding-on mini-lessons, remind your students that they too can add on to their pieces and ask them what is the first thing they need to do before they can add on. Children will respond that they have to reread what they have already written. You may want to ask your students who want to add on to raise their hands and partner them up so that they can do the rereading with a partner who is also adding on.

Thinking Aloud about How You Write

When we write, we do not read aloud what we are writing—but we do "think aloud" about how we are writing. For younger children, you may make very basic statements, such as:

> I will use my finger to make sure I put a good space between the words and make it easy to read.
>
> I am at the end of that sentence, so I put my period here.

With older students, think aloud and model more sophisticated thinking, such as:

> My sentence is a question, so I am using a question mark.
>
> When my cat had eight kittens, I was really surprised. This sentence deserves an exclamation mark.
>
> I am writing about the second spoke on my web, so I will start a new paragraph.

For students of any age, think aloud about how you use the words in the room, words that rhyme with words you can spell, and stretching out words to spell.

> I can spell *beautiful* because it is on the word wall.
>
> *Reptile* is on our animal vocabulary board.
>
> I want to write *spray* and I can spell *play*, so I can use the rhyming pattern.
>
> *Disappointed* is a word I can spell now but I would have had to sound it out when I was your age. I will put down the letters I hear and then circle it so that I remember to check on that spelling if this is a piece I decide to publish.

For children of all ages, think aloud as you decide what to write next.

Let's see, I wrote that Gorlab was a golden retriever whose favorite thing to retrieve was socks. What else should I tell about Gorlab?

If you have made a Five Finger Plan, cluster, web, or Double Bubble to plan your writing, be explicit in how it helps you organize.

Now, I've written about how monkeys and chimpanzees are alike. I should write a paragraph telling about the special things about chimps that are in the chimps part of the circle.

Thinking aloud lets students in on how you write. As the year progresses and you focus your mini-lessons on revising and editing, your think-alouds will focus on more sophisticated writing elements. Throughout the year, continue to use think-alouds to allow your students to hear you talking about what you are doing while writing and let your students listen in on that little voice in your head.

Sharing

Sharing writing is always important but it is particularly important early in the year. Students get ideas from the writing shared by others and everyone likes to share the things that are important in their lives. When the writing time is over, circle your students and let volunteers share what they wrote. (You may want to have them stand in a circle as they share because they have been sitting while they write and they may be "antsy.") If they have drawn a picture, let them show their picture and tell what they have written. Model the kinds of questions and connecting comments you want students to use as they respond to each other's writing. You may want to let each student who shares call on a friend to tell something that person liked or to ask a question. You can make sure the comments are positive by requiring the responder to start the sentence with "What I liked about that was . . ."

The most important rule to keep in mind about sharing is that it is not required. Students share only if they volunteer to share. This is not usually a problem with younger children, all of whom often want to share. To keep to your time limits, you may need to write down the names of students who wanted to share today but didn't get to and make sure they get to share first tomorrow if they volunteer.

What If?

What if Some Students Never Volunteer to Share?

With older students who have not had good experiences with writing, only a few students may be willing to share for the first several days. If only two students volunteer to share, let those two share and call on a friend to tell something he or she liked. Most teachers find that when no criticism is made of the writing and only positive responses are given by the teacher and other students, more and more resistant writers will be willing to share. In fact, you may quickly end up with too many volunteers and need to start a list of those who get to share first tomorrow if they choose to.

Looking Back
What Do I Do Once I Have Them Writing?

Once you have your students off to a successful start:

- Teach a variety of mini-lessons on choosing a topic.
- Teach some mini-lessons on planning, expanding beyond one sentence, and adding on.
- Think aloud about how you write, letting them listen to that little voice in your head.
- Let volunteers share and model good questions and connection comments.

Chapter 3

Spelling Matters!

Spelling is the biggest roadblock to writing. Glance at a piece of writing and the misspelled words pop right out at you.

Younger students often think they can't write if they can't spell all the words. Older students sometimes refuse to write if teachers don't spell words for them, or they write only what they can spell, rather than what they want to tell!

We teach spelling, of course, but we often see the same words spelled correctly on the morning spelling test misspelled during the afternoon writing time. If a passing grade on the spelling test is what matters, then struggling spellers may learn the words for the test and promptly forget them after completing the test.

Most teachers are terribly conflicted about what to do about spelling when students are writing. They realize that writers are not going to be able to spell all the words they need, but teachers are afraid that if they encourage their writers to spell words as best they can, their students will never learn to spell the words correctly. Some teachers fly around the room as their students write, spelling words for students as they need them. In these classrooms, many children sit with their hands raised waiting for the teacher to get to them and provide a spelling before they continue writing. Sometimes, by the time the teacher gets to the students with the raised hands, these students have forgotten what word they were trying to spell! In classrooms in which teachers fly from desk to desk providing spelling help, no one will attempt to spell words they are unsure of and children will get very little written during the writing time.

Older students are often unwilling to seek spelling help. They know they are supposed to be able to spell most words—but they can't. These older students who don't spell well are often the ones who declare they "ain't got nothing to write about" when the truth is they have plenty they would like to tell but can't spell the words that match their thoughts. Some clever older students have figured out how to "beat the system." They write the same kind of thing every day, using only the words they can spell.

The Mall

I went to the mall. I went with my brother. We played games. We walked around. We went in some cool stores. It was fun at the mall.

Most teachers recognize *The Mall* as the type of boring piece they see day in and day out from struggling writers asked to write on their own topics. Where are the details? The descriptive language? If this student were talking to his friends about his trip to the mall, it might sound like this:

Jason and I had an awesome time at the new mall Saturday afternoon. First, we rode the escalators down to the first level. That's where the game store is.

They have every game you want! Then, we rode the escalators up to the top to the food court. They have 10 different restaurants! I ate Mexican and he ate Japanese. We split a cinnamon roll for dessert. Then we went down to the second level and shopped for Steelers' paraphernalia at the sports stores. Just wait 'til you see my way-cool sweatshirt!

If he can include all this detail and rich descriptive language in telling, why is his writing so painfully bland? This student is writing what he can spell—not what he can tell. By using only simple words he is sure how to spell, he eliminates the risk of misspelling a word. General nouns—*brother, games, stores*—eliminate the risk that a noun might be one of those "proper" ones that need a capital letter. Short sentences can't possibly be in violation of any punctuation rules and need those confusing commas and quotation marks. This clever struggling writer has figured out how to produce perfect writing—every time!

Spelling matters greatly to writing. Unless you provide some spelling supports for your students and find ways to make "best attempt" spellings acceptable in first drafts, your struggling students won't write or will write simple, boring, painful, "perfect" text. In this chapter, we will outline a variety of ways you can provide spelling support for writing in your classrooms and liberate your students so they can write what they want to tell—not just what they can spell!

What If?

What if My Students Won't Write if I Don't Spell Words for Them?

Kids like to spell everything correctly and they would like us to be their spelling support. Once you start, they will never let you stop. Point out places in the room where they can find words. Help them stretch out words and praise their effort, telling them you couldn't have stretched that word nearly as well when you were their age! Have them circle these words and assure them you will help them with correct spelling if this is a piece they publish.

If they whine that last year's teacher spelled words for them, tell them, "Third-grade (or whatever grade you teach) teachers aren't allowed to do that!"

If you have been spelling words for them all year and it is about to be February, have the "How things change in February" talk, including "Teachers are no longer allowed to spell words for you once February comes."

The Word Wall-Writing Connection

Many varieties of word walls can be found decorating classroom walls but did you ever wonder who did the first word wall? A word wall as a spelling support to writing was invented by one of the authors, Pat, when she was working with a small rural school in 1975. The first spelling word wall ever was constructed in a second-grade classroom in which almost all the children spelled words exactly as they sounded.

October

October is my favrit munth. The levs ar prite culers. Thay fall of the tres. Holowen cums in October. I lik to go trik or tret and git lots uv cande. Wut is yor favrit munth?

Could you read the October piece typical of the writing done by the second-graders in this class? Here was a whole class full of students who had learned some phonics in first grade and who used phonics to spell words exactly as they sounded. Their teacher could read their writing easily but was appalled by their spelling. This kind of writing demonstrates why many teachers are afraid to let children spell words as best they can.

In English, many of the most frequently used words are not spelled the way they sound. Some of the most commonly written words in the "October" piece include *favorite, are, pretty, they, off, come, like, get, of, what,* and *your*. Of the 36 words in this piece, these 11 words are common words used day in and day out in the writing of most children and are not spelled the way they sound. The second-grade teacher in this class and Pat decided to gradually add common words such as these to one of the bulletin boards in the room, to provide daily practice in spelling these words and then to hold the students accountable for spelling these word wall words correctly in their writing. Word wall was conceived and born in that second-grade classroom.

It was not quick or easy to change the way those second-graders spelled common words such as *what, they, are, of,* and *like*. One of the many functions of the brain—wondrous organ that it is—includes automaticity, or making something automatic after someone has done that thing many times. For example, when you spell a word correctly in your writing several times, your brain learns that this is the correct spelling, and soon you can spell that word automatically—without any of your precious, conscious attention being used to think about the spelling of that word. That is the good news! The bad news is that if you spell a word incorrectly many times—*wut, thay, ar, uv, lik*—your brain makes that spelling automatic. Because those second-graders had spelled these words the way they sounded almost every day in their writing—the spelling had become automatic. When someone does something automatically, it is hard to change because the person is not aware she or he is doing it. The purpose of a word wall is to teach children to automatically spell the words they use most frequently in their writing. Ideally, children in first grade would have and use a word wall to spell common irregular words correctly when they first start to write. Teachers of older children who misspell common words can use the word wall strategies to "reprogram" their students' brains with the automatic correct spelling of common words.

How to Do a Word Wall as Spelling Support for Writing

In many classrooms, students know that when writing first drafts, they should spell a word as best they can unless that word is on the word wall. The teacher chooses words to place on the wall that are commonly used in writing and that students are going to misspell if they spell them the way they sound. The students practice the word wall words by "cheering" (explained on page 39) for those words and writing them. Most importantly, when students write, the teacher reminds them that the word wall words are often tricky, and they should glance at the word wall if they are unsure about how to spell a word wall word because "word wall words must be spelled correctly in everything you write!"

Choosing the Words

If you keep in mind what you want your word wall to accomplish for your students, choosing the words to add to the wall is easy. The word wall should include words your students use frequently in their writing and that they are likely to misspell if these words are not on the word wall. Look in the first-draft writing of your students and word wall possibilities will jump out at you. In many classrooms, the first five words added to the wall are some of the words in the "October" piece. If many of your students commonly misspell *what, they, of, off,* and *come,* these are perfect words to begin with because we all use them in our writing almost every time we write. Other very common words many teachers add early to their word walls include *from, have, said, want, because, were, where,* and *very.* Many students write about friends and family so word walls often contain common, tricky words such as *family, friend, brother, sister, cousin, aunt,* and *uncle.* Commonly used adjectives are often not easily spelled and many word walls contain words such as *favorite, pretty, beautiful, nice, fantastic,* and *awesome.*

In most classrooms, students misspell common homophones—*to, too, two; their, there, they're; your, you're; here, hear; right, write; new, knew;* and *no, know*. When you add homophones such as these to the wall, put a clue on all but one of them so that your students can remember which word has which meaning. Often, teachers use the clue "2" to indicate the meaning of *two*, "too big also" to indicate both meanings of *too; to* is "the other one." You may want to underline the <u>ear</u> in *hear*—a convenient clue. Opposites—*right* (wrong); *no* (yes); *new* (old)—are also clues students find helpful in determining the correct spelling of homophones.

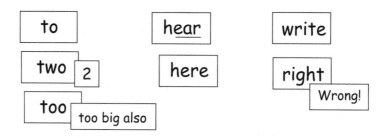

Contractions also present spelling problems for many writers and are thus added to the word wall. Some contractions are also homophones, and clues are needed to help students distinguish these. The <u>here</u> in *there* is underlined as the clue that t-h-e-r-e is the *there* that means the opposite of *here*.

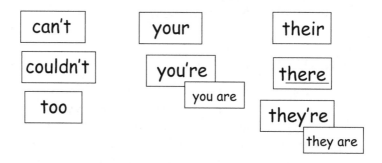

When adding words to the wall, place them under the letter they begin with so that your students can quickly find them when they are writing. Because many of the words look a lot like other common irregular words (*of, off; want, went, what; were, where*), use colored paper or index cards for the words making sure to put confusable words and homophones on different colors. Add the words gradually— no more than five each week—and sponge up otherwise wasted snatches of time by practicing the words.

Practicing the Words

Once the words are on the wall, you need to provide students opportunities to practice these words—particularly if the words you are adding are words students have learned to spell automatically wrong. Remember that the brain makes things automatic after a person has done them the same way several times. To reprogram the brain from incorrect spellings to correct spellings, students need many opportunities to practice spelling the words correctly. To practice the words, we cheer them and write them. Cheering the words provides students with an auditory-rhythmic route to remembering the correct spelling. Writing the words provides a kinesthetic route.

How teachers lead their students to cheer words is easy to understand if you see it and hard to describe in words. The most important thing for you to remember about cheering the words is that you are trying to provide your students with an auditory-rhythmic route to storing and retrieving the correct spelling. You can lead the children to clap the letters as they say them.

> Let's clap the spelling of *because*.
>
> Students clap and cheer *because* three times.
>
> "b-e-c-a-u-s-e, because!" "b-e-c-a-u-s-e, because!"
> "b-e-c-a-u-s-e, because!"

Other actions help the rhythmic cheering.

> Let's snap the spelling of *from*.
>
> Students snap their fingers and cheer *from* three times.
>
> "f-r-o-m, from!" "f-r-o-m, from!" "f-r-o-m, from!"

> Let's stomp the spelling of the *there* that is the opposite of *here*.
>
> Students stomp their feet and cheer *there* three times.
>
> "t-h-e-r-e, there!" ""t-h-e-r-e, there!" "t-h-e-r-e, there!"

If you are having trouble imagining what this auditory-rhythmic practice looks and sounds like, just think of a basketball or football game and hear the crowds cheering their favorite teams to victory. Your role as teacher is to be the cheerleader and get your students excited about being victorious in learning to spell these tricky words.

Although cheering the words is more fun than writing the words, it is important that you also provide some opportunities for students to write these words because writing the words correctly can give them a kinesthetic or muscle route to storing and retrieving the correct spelling. You will not accomplish anything by having them write the words five times each because clever children will accomplish this task quickly by writing the first letter five times and then the second letter five times—and so on. This does nothing to help put the right letters in the right order in their brains. Also, you want your students to access the correct spellings when they are actually writing. Children of all ages enjoy riddles, and many teachers provide writing practice with the word wall words by creating some simple riddles in which students must decide which word fits in the sentence. The teacher gives the clues and the sentence with the missing word orally. Students write only the word that correctly completes the sentence.

> Let's practice some of our word wall words with some word wall riddles. I have five riddles for you today. Number your paper from 1 to 5. Here is my first riddle. "I start with *w*. I have 4 letters. I am missing from this sentence: Jason and Liz _____ absent yesterday."

Students write *were* next to number 1 on their papers and you continue with riddle #2.

> "I start with *w*. I have 4 letters. I am missing from this sentence: I wonder _____ Carlton will get for his birthday."

Students write *what* next to number 2 and you continue with riddle #3.

> "I start with *t*. I have 5 letters. I am missing from this sentence: Maria, William, and Girard brought _____ lunch boxes today."

Students write *their* next to #3 and you continue with two more riddles.

The riddles sound simple but all the children can "solve" them and they enjoy the immediate feeling of success this gives them. Using the names of your students in the sentences greatly increases their engagement and enjoyment of this simple activity. When your students get good at this, you may want to assign five students each day to compose a riddle. Give each child one index card with the word you want reviewed. Have them write out their clues on the back of the index card so you can make sure the sentence works. Of course, check the sentences also to make sure nothing negative is said about any student.

WORDO

By far the favorite word wall review activity is WORDO. The quick version uses nine squares and you can have multiple winners playing the game for just a few minutes. Make a 3 × 3 template of nine squares with WORDO written in the middle.

Choose 8 word wall words you want to review. Write these words on index cards as your students write them in the squares. When the eight words are written, shuffle your cards and show students the first word. Have them say the word and cover it on their sheet (using buttons, pennies, small sticky notes, etc.). When someone has three words in a row—vertical, horizontal or diagonal—they should shout, "WORDO!" If they have the words spelled correctly on their sheets, declare them the winners. Everyone clears their sheets as you shuffle all your cards and another round of play begins. WORDO is a fast-paced game that students of all ages love to play. They quickly learn that they *must* have the words spelled correctly on their sheets. As they write, see, say, and cover the words, they are getting additional practice with these important words.

	WORDO	

from	didn't	they
there	WORDO	their
two	wouldn't	they're

What About My Advanced Writers?

Even your best writers probably have some common words they misspell. English is a very complex language from a spelling standpoint. Your best writers probably began writing at an earlier age and they may have spelled many words in the logical but incorrect way. Many wonderful writers confuse the common homophones—*there, their, they're; its, it's.* Putting commonly misspelled words on a word wall is often as helpful to your advanced writers as it is for your struggling writers.

Model How to Use the Word Wall While Writing

The most important thing about a word wall is that you want students to spell these words correctly in their writing. From the day you put the first five words on the wall, model and think aloud as you are writing in your mini-lesson how the word wall helps you spell these tricky words correctly. Plan to use at least one of the word wall words in your writing and as you begin to write that word, look up at the word wall, smile, and then say something like,

Because is tricky but I know I can spell it correctly by checking it on our word wall.

Each day, during your mini-lessons, think aloud about how helpful the word wall is.

I need to spell the word *their* and I don't mean the opposite of *here* or *they are*, so it must be the other one I need.

I am going to write *couldn't* and the word wall will help me make sure I put the apostrophe in the right place.

We just added *awesome* to the word wall and *awesome* is exactly the word I need to explain the winning shot at the buzzer.

As your word wall grows, don't take your students' attention away from your writing by looking up at the wall as your write every word wall word. Just focus on one word—preferably a recently added one—each time and model for your students how helpful the word wall is in allowing you to spell tricky words quickly and correctly.

Hold Students Accountable for Word Wall Words in All Writing

From the day you put the first words on the wall, be alert to word wall words misspelled in your students' writing. If you have chosen the words to put on your wall by looking for commonly misspelled words in their writing, expect to continue to see these words misspelled for a few weeks. Remember that the brain has practiced the incorrect spelling many times and has made this spelling automatic. When your students are writing and they write *thay, cum,* or *wut*, they are doing this automatically—without conscious attention.

When you see a misspelled word wall word, don't say anything. Just quickly write *WW* above that word. *WW* means "This word is on the word wall; fix it!" Do this while circulating when students are first-draft writing. Do this when you see a word wall word misspelled in a math journal. Do this when you see a word wall word misspelled any place and any time. Before long, as your students begin to write a word wall word in the automatic but incorrect way, a little voice inside their heads will say, "WW" and they will fix it on their own. You have now accomplished your goal of reprogramming their brains—at least for that word! In the "Football" example, *favorite* and *friend* are on the word wall, so they are marked with a *WW*. *Every* and *touchdown* are not on the word wall, so of course they are not marked. The teacher might decide to add *every* to the word wall, however, because it is a commonly misspelled word. *Touchdown* is not a common enough word to be put on the word wall.

Football

Football is my favrit sport. I play football evry week. I play with

my frends at the park. Last week, I made a tuch down.

A little over 100 words comprise 50 percent **of the** words **we** write **every** time **we** write. The bold words in the previous sentence are a few of these high-frequency words and they do indeed account for half the words in this sentence. Many of the most common words are not spelled the way they sound. Students are going to use these common words every day when they write. If they spell them the way they sound, they will spell those words wrong and this incorrect spelling will become automatic. By gradually adding these common words to your word wall, practicing them by cheering and writing, modeling how helpful the word wall is as you write, and holding your students accountable for the correct spelling of word wall words, you can be sure that all your students will learn to automatically spell these common, tricky words correctly! Teachers who do word walls consistently don't worry about encouraging their students to spell it as best they can on first drafts. Words such as *touchdown, leprechaun,* and *Plymouth* are not written often enough for them to become automatic the way they sound (*tuchdown, leprekon, plimuth*). If, in addition to your word wall, you compile a chart of timely words each month, you can enable your students to spell seasonal/holiday words correctly when they write.

The Monthly Word Chart

Imagine that it is the first day of November. You begin the writing time by going over to where a chart labeled October Words is displayed. Your students quickly tell what some of their favorite *October* words were—*football, Bulldogs, Halloween, trick or treat, festival*—and you remove the chart. In its place, you attach a blank chart and quickly label it *November Words*.

> It's a new month and we're going to need some new words to write about things that happen and things we do in November. Who has a word we might need in our writing this month?

Your students, who have done September and October charts, quickly contribute ideas and you record them. One student suggests "football" and another student objects, "We had that word in October." You write football on the chart and say,

> Some words are only needed one month but November is a very important month for football so we will add it to this list too.

In eight minutes, the students have brainstormed a long list that you have recorded. The chart is almost, but not quite, full of words and you remind the students that you will add more words until the chart is full if they think of other important November words.

```
November
football  pumpkin pie
Thanksgiving  pilgrims
feast  snow
turkey  windy
parade  fall
stuffing  festival
  vote
leaves  rake harvest
colorful  holiday
```

After beginning the *November Words* chart, you explain that the chart will help us spell lots of words and that it might give us ideas for topics to write about.

> In fact, as you were thinking of words, I remembered something we did when I was your age to celebrate Thanksgiving.

Next, you write a "When I was Your Age" tale sharing a memory from your childhood sparked by the words on the chart. (Sometimes referred to as *Your Age Tales*, these always begin with the familiar words, When I was your age, . . .) Today you write two paragraphs, glancing occasionally at the just brainstormed chart of November words to spell some words.

My Unexpected Starring Role in the Thanksgiving Play

When I was your age, our class was chosen to do the Thanksgiving play. We all got roles and I was one of the pilgrim children who ran around playing tag and helping the women cook. I was excited about the play but a little disappointed that I didn't have a speaking part.

It was the morning of the play. The auditorium was filling up with parents and we were getting into our costumes. Our teacher, Mrs. Donahue, was very nervous but trying not to show it. Suddenly, Rita Terranova, who had the starring role, threw up! Her parents who were there for the play took her home. Mrs. Donahue looked like she might throw up too. "I don't know what we will do," she said. "Rita has the biggest part and no one else knows her lines." "I do," I said in a quiet voice. "I know everyone's parts!" Mrs. Donahue didn't believe me but she had me say the first couple and then she knew. "O.K., Patricia, you are our new star. Put on Rita's costume. It's show time!"

> I have a lot more to tell you about our class play and my starring role in the play so I will be adding on to this piece tomorrow.

The students, as always, urge you to continue writing but you refuse to cut into their writing time and you get them started with their writing. Many—but not all—write Thanksgiving or other November related pieces and you are delighted to see students glancing at the November chart to spell some of the words they need to tell their own stories.

Teachers who regularly lead students to brainstorm needed words for each month will tell you that they can't imagine how they taught writing before they began the monthly charts. Children of all ages like to write about holidays and other seasonal happenings in their lives. Combined with the high-frequency words on the word wall, the monthly chart enables all students to quickly and correctly spell the majority of the words they are writing. Students of all ages are more willing to spell words as best they can when they know they are spelling most of the words correctly—particularly if you model how to "phonic spell" some words and teach your students to circle words they know are not spelled correctly. Once your students are using the word wall and the monthly chart as spelling supports, it is time to do some mini-lessons on phonics spelling.

Why Not?
Why Not Just Have Them Use the Dictionary?

Once you have taught students how to use the dictionary to determine the correct spelling of a word, you should encourage students to use the dictionary during the editing process to fix the spelling of any words they know are not spelled correctly. But, it is probably not wise to let them look up words in the dictionary while they are doing first-draft writing. If allowed to check spellings in the dictionary while writing, many students will spend all their time looking up words and get very little written. While they are looking for the word, they often lose their train of thought and forget what they intended to write. If you teach older students and you have taught them how to find correct spellings in the dictionary, you may want to give them a few minutes when they finish writing to look up any words they did not know how to spell. The important thing is not to let the dictionary interrupt their ideas or become the excuse for producing very little writing.

How I Would Have Spelled It
When I Was Your Age

If you want your students to spell words as best they can, you must show them how to do this. As you write each day in your mini-lesson, you should spell most words correctly, modeling how the word wall, monthly chart, and other print in the room help you spell correctly.

> I'm so glad we added *shouldn't* to the word wall. That is a very tricky contraction.
>
> I am not sure I could have spelled *leprechaun* if we hadn't put it on our March Words.
>
> Our Dinosaur bulletin board will help me spell lots of the names of the dinosaurs.

You also need to stretch out a few words, putting down letters for the sounds you hear. Many teachers are uncomfortable "pretending" they can't spell a word. One solution is to tell your students, as you begin to stretch out a word and "sound spell" it:

> I can spell *frightened* now but this is probably how I would have spelled it when I was your age.

When you model phonics spelling and imply that this is how you would have done it at their age (and you probably would have if anyone had let you!), your students are willing to write words they have not yet learned to spell.

Another trick teachers use to show their students how to phonic spell words is to circle each word they have stretched out to spell. As they circle the word, they say something like,

> I am going to circle *fritend* because I stretched it out and it doesn't look right and I want to remember to get help spelling *frightened* if this is a piece I publish.

The message you want to give your students about spelling is that they should use all the spelling support in the room to spell words as correctly as they can. When they are trying to spell a word they know they can't spell and they can't quickly find it in the room, they should stretch out that word and spell it as best they can. When they have stretched out a word, they should circle it because when they publish pieces, they get help to fix all the spelling.

> On Saturday I was visiting my mom. Suddenly, it started to rain really hard. The wind blew some of the deck chairs over. We were watching TV and the program was interrupted by a weather buletin. A tornado had been spotted and was heading right for my mom's naborhood. We went downstairs and both scrunched into the closet. We grabbed the pillows and blankets off the shelf and covered ourselves with them. We could hear the wind and rain pelting the house and we were both very friend. After what seemed like hours but was probably only 5 minutes, the storm stopped and we went outside. There were sticks and limbs down but no real damage. As suddenly as the rain had started, the sun came out and my mom and I started cleaning up the yard.

Once you are modeling the spelling and circling of words you weren't sure how to spell, you need to reinforce this with your students when they are writing. Remember that you don't spell words for students when they are doing a first draft but you do remind them to use all the visible spelling supports in the room and you do help them stretch out and circle words they need that are not in the room.

As you circulate during the writing time and see "stopped" children, stop and say something like:

What are you trying to say?

(Student responds that he is trying to spell *Super Bowl*.)

Look at the words on our January chart. I bet you will find *Super Bowl* there.

To another student who has written *Wake Forest de:*

What are you trying to say about my favorite team, Wake Forest?

(Student responds that he is writing that Wake demolished Duke in Saturday's game.)

Demolished—what a wonderful word. Let's stretch it out.

(Teacher helps student say *demolished* slowly and student writes *demulished*.)

You are very close. Circle your spelling to remind yourself to get help with that spelling if this is a piece you decide to publish.

Why Not?
Why Not Just Spell the Words for Them?

If the idea of coaching students to use room spelling resources to spell words displayed in the room and helping them to stretch out words they need that are not available in the room is new to you, you might be asking, "Wouldn't it be quicker just to spell the words for them?" The answer: "Yes, it would, but then they would be dependent on you for spelling help." Once you have your students writing willingly and able to handle their own spelling issues, you are going to want to spend your time while students write holding individual conferences with students. Coaching your students to know exactly what to do about spelling frees you for the much more important job of helping students revise and edit.

Some teachers like to post a chart in the room to remind (and reassure) their students about how they expect them to spell words in first draft writing.

What to Do about Spelling

1. Search the room.

2. Say the word slowly.

3. Write letters for the sounds you hear.

4. Read the word you wrote.

5. Circle the word.

Looking Back

Spelling Matters!

Spelling matters but what matters more is getting your students to write what they want to tell—not just what they can spell. To improve student spelling and remove spelling as a roadblock to writing:

- Add common misspelled words to a classroom word wall.
- Practice word wall words by cheering and writing them.
- Require that word wall words be spelled correctly in all writing.
- Each month, have students contribute words to a monthly word chart.
- Model in your mini-lessons how the word wall and other words displayed in the room help you spell many words correctly.
- Model stretching out a few words you couldn't spell "when you were their age." Circle these words to show you know this is *not* the correct spelling.
- Encourage your students to use vivid words that tell what they want to tell, not just words they can spell. Have them circle any words they think are not spelled correctly.
- Assure your students that when they publish pieces, you will help them fix the spelling so that everyone can easily read their writing.

Chapter 4

Think-Writes: Writing to Learn across the Curriculum

For most of us, the writing we did in school was all about showing what we thought and what we had learned. If we wrote at all for our science, social studies, and math classes, it was probably a test or a report.

This writing was almost always given a grade—sometimes two grades, one for the content and one for the writing. In this chapter, we want you to try to think outside the box of your own experience and consider the possibility that writing might help students think as well as learn—rather than just assess their thinking and learning.

To begin changing your point of view about writing, think about the writing you do in your "out of school" life. When asked what writing they do outside the school context, many teachers' first responses are that they don't do any, but that response indicates a very narrow concept of writing.

Have you made any lists lately? Some of us are more compulsive list makers but almost everyone makes some lists. In our house, we keep a large index card on the refrigerator to help us make our trips to the grocery store more efficient. If you put out the last roll of paper towels or use the last egg, you are expected to add that to the list. Whoever's turn it is to grocery shop (not the favorite kind of shopping for anyone in our house) takes this list and adds to it items needed for the week's meals. We also keep "to-do" lists. A productive day is when more things get crossed off the to-do list than get added.

In addition to lists, many of us write reminder notes to ourselves. A glance at the refrigerator might reveal sticky notes reminding us of haircut appointments, upcoming birthdays, and the Tuesday morning arrival of the termite inspector. Some more organized people write these reminders in a planner or date book. That works fine if you remember where you put the date book and to check it regularly! Regardless of where we write them, most of us record appointments and events with dates and times and these reminders help us be where we need to be.

Lists and reminders are a daily part of many of our lives. There are other kinds of writing we do on a less regular basis. Sometimes we are pondering a tough decision—which car to buy, whether to go to the mountains or the coast for our summer getaway, whether to hunt for a different job. As we are thinking about this, we might find ourselves making a pro/con list. Writing down the reasons to do or not do certain things helps clarify our thinking and make a decision. When contemplating the purchase of a house, for example, you might list the pros and cons to help you decide if the time is right.

Reasons to Buy This Year	Reasons to Wait
Housing prices will probably go up next year.	We probably could sell our house for more next year.
We're going to need a new roof soon.	My husband might lose his job.
Our next door neighbor is a pill!	We could save for a bigger down payment.
Our credit rating is the best it's ever been.	We could look around more to decide where we really want to live.

Writing can also be a catharsis. Grief counselors often suggest that their clients describe in writing the accident, illness, loss, betrayal, or other devastating event as a way of beginning the healing process.

> The earliest memories I have of my grandmother were when I was four and went to live with her for three months. My mother had been in a terrible accident and she spent a long time in the hospital and later in a rehabilitation center. My father couldn't take care of me because he had a long commute to his job. Granny was so gentle and kind. I loved the smell of her house. There were always flowers in a vase somewhere and she was a wonderful cook. After my mother came home, I moved back home. But Granny and I were always close. When I received the call last week that Granny had had a massive stroke, it occurred to me that she might die, and I let my principal know that I wouldn't be at school for several days. I was due to fly there the next morning when my uncle called the second time to say she had passed away. Oh, how I miss being able to call her to talk about the least thing! I am grieving hard for her, but I am surprised that I also feel tremendous gratitude. What if I had never known her?

What all these kinds of writing have in common is that they are not writing that we are doing for others. We write lists, reminders, pro/con reasons, and descriptions of personal anguish for ourselves—to help us think about, remember, sort out, clarify, and learn. To distinguish this writing from writing meant to communicate with others, we have coined the term *think-writes*. Think-writes are single-draft writing that help us think and learn. In this chapter, we will describe how you can use think-writes in your classroom to engage your students more deeply in thinking about what they are learning.

Think-Writes to Activate Prior Knowledge

All teachers know that in order to learn new information, students must access what they already know about a topic. Only when prior knowledge has been activated can students make the connections that result in new learning and increased prior knowledge. Think-writes can make your efforts at prior knowledge activation more productive for all your students.

Imagine that your learning focus for a lesson is on presidents. This focus on presidents might be part of your social studies curriculum on famous Americans, or part of your celebration of Presidents' Day, or preparation for a biography unit that is part of your reading curriculum. In many classrooms, this focus on presidents would begin with the teacher asking the class for input.

> Today we are going to start learning about some of our nation's presidents. Who knows something about presidents?

Hands will be raised and various students will contribute what they know. There are problems, however, with this typical classroom method of activating prior knowledge. The first problem has to do with whose hands fly up. Some hands are always raised and others are rarely or never raised. What prior knowledge is being activated in the minds of the students whose hands are not raised? Surely, they know something about presidents. Why do some hands almost never fly into the air? Equally problematic (and more annoying!) are the students whose hands always fly up and then when they are the first person called on ask, "What was the question?"

Contrast this familiar classroom scenario with a classroom in which you use a think-write to help students activate their prior knowledge about presidents.

> Today we are going to start learning about some of our nation's presidents. Take a piece of scratch paper and write down everything you know about presidents. If you think you know something but you aren't sure, write it down anyway and we will try to find out. You have two minutes. Go!

While your students write, you stand in front of the class and watch the clock, timing the students for exactly two minutes. Most of your students will write as fast as they can, trying to "beat the clock" and write down many things. Your students no longer ask you to spell things—as they did the first few times you did these think-writes because they know what the answer will be.

> Spell it as best you can. This writing is just for you to get your thoughts down. No one else needs to read it so as long as you know what you wrote, we're good.

When exactly two minutes have passed, you say,

> Stop! Pens down! Who has something they want to share?

Every hand is raised. You call first on a student who may not have much prior knowledge and that student proudly responds, "George Washington."

Good thinking. George Washington was our first president.

You continue to call on students and affirm their responses.

Yes, the president is the head of our nation.

Yes, presidents get elected every four years.

Sometimes, you ask a follow-up question.

Yes, Abraham Lincoln was a president. Does anyone know how Abraham Lincoln died?

The president does live in the White House. Who knows where the White House is?

Good thinking. We did have two presidents named George Bush. We also had two other presidents with the same name. Does anyone have an idea who they might be?

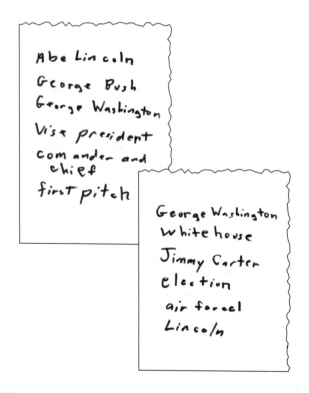

Another student volunteers, "George Washington" and you remind everyone that we need to listen and not repeat ideas. You ask that student if he has anything on his list that hasn't been said. When students volunteer information that is clearly incorrect, you correct that information but affirm the response of the student.

> Benjamin Franklin was never president but he played a very important role in our government. Can anyone tell us what Benjamin Franklin did?

When no more hands are raised, you compliment your students on how much they already know about presidents and tell them that they will be learning many more interesting presidential facts and trivia in the coming days.

Think-writes to activate prior knowledge increase student engagement and motivation. Your most able students will see it as a kind of race and will want to write as many ideas as they can in the two minutes. Struggling students who may be reluctant to raise their hands are much more confident when they have had two minutes to think and when the teacher is somewhat affirming of even a wrong answer or a misconception. Using think-writes forces teachers to do something we know we need to do—but often find ourselves not doing. When we give them two minutes to write down ideas, we are forced to "wait" while they write. Both quantity and quality of student responses increase when we give students' wait time. Two-minute think-writes make students think and teachers wait!

Once you start using think-writes, you will wonder how you taught without them. You can use think-writes to activate prior knowledge during math.

> We are going to be learning more about measurement this week. You have two minutes to write everything you think you already know about measurement. Go!
>
> Our new math topic is fractions. I know you already know a lot about fractions. Take a piece of scratch paper and write down what you know. You have two minutes. Go!

Science topics also can be introduced with two-minute think-writes.

> Our new science topic is on natural resources. Do you know any? What do you think you know about natural resources? You have two minutes. Go!
>
> Rocks is our science topic for the week. I know you know things about rocks. Let's see how much rock knowledge you can write down in two minutes. Go!

You may even uncover some science misconceptions that are part of your students' prior knowledge. If someone tells you something you are sure is incorrect, make a mental note of that and respond by saying something like,

> A lot of people think that—but we are going to find out that it actually works quite differently.

Here are some two-minute think-writes used to access prior knowledge in social studies.

> What holiday do we celebrate in November? Right! Thanksgiving will soon be here. I know you know a lot about Thanksgiving. Grab some scratch paper and get those brains thinking. You have two minutes. Go!
>
> Immigration is our social studies topic. I am not sure how much you know about immigration but we will soon find out. You have two minutes. Go!

Notice in these examples that the teacher instructs the students to use "scratch paper." Scratch paper is paper we collect from around the copying machine and tear into quarters. We always have this scratch paper available on student desks or tables. This scratch paper is essential to successful two-minute think-writes for several reasons. First, it often takes a whole class of students more than two minutes to "get out a piece of paper." In two minutes, the think-write is done. Second, scratch paper is unintimidating. No one asks if they need to "head their paper" or if "this counts for the grade" when jotting down thoughts on a small scrap of paper. Finally, we are recycling paper that would have been thrown away and the children are not wasting perfectly good whole pieces of notebook paper!

It is also important to specify and stick to the time limit. Two minutes is plenty of time for students to recall and jot down most of what they know. Students who don't know much don't get too squirmy in two minutes and students who know a lot enjoy racing to write down an impressive array of facts before the time is up.

Think-Writes for Prediction

In addition to making connections, thinking often involves making predictions or guesses about what we will learn or what is going to happen. Psychologists call predicting *forward inferencing* and suggest that by making predictions, the brain is creating slots for the new information and deciding ahead of time where to store it. Prediction is also a powerful tool for engaging students. In real life, people often use prediction to entice listeners to attend to what they are saying. In the Cunningham house, we often have conversations that go something like this:

Pat (arriving home from work): NPR had some frightening statistics on the dropout rate today. What percent of students in our 17 largest cities are not finishing high school in four years?

Jim: I don't know. How many?

Pat: Guess!

Jim: Probably a lot. How many?

Pat: You have to guess first.

Jim (reluctantly): OK. At least 40 percent.

Pat: 50 percent! Half the kids—and that counts only those who actually enroll in ninth grade! Now, how many drop out in Detroit?

Jim (knowing Pat won't tell him until he guesses): I don't know. Maybe 60 percent?

Pat: 75 percent! That's what the last 10 years of federal control and accountability has wrought for our neediest kids! Shocking—but sadly, not surprising!

Prediction is a way of grabbing attention and engaging the mind for what will come. You will find numerous opportunities during your school day to use prediction think-writes. Science is a fertile area for prediction. In fact, prediction is one of the science processes teachers want all students to do regularly. Imagine that you are teaching a science unit on magnets and electricity and want your students to make some predictions and then test those predictions.

Boys and girls, we are going to continue our unit on magnets and electricity today. In just a few minutes, you are going to get into your teams and test some materials and see if the magnets will attract them. Before we test them, let's make some predictions. Grab a sheet of scratch paper and number it from 1 to 6. Next to number 1, write ruler. *Then write either* attract *or* not *to show your prediction. Will the ruler be attracted to the magnet?*

The prediction think-write continues as you hold up each object your students are going to test. Students write the name of the object and their guess of attract or not next to each. Some students are hesitant to guess and claim they don't know (just as Jim was hesitant to guess the percentage of dropouts). You push them, however, by saying something like:

> You're not supposed to know. That's what a guess is. When you test them, you will change any guesses to the correct answers. Make your best guess. I'm not going to let you join your team to test the objects until you have made a prediction for each.

Prediction is a powerful motivator but students are often afraid of being wrong. When they learn that you don't care if they are wrong or right and that they are expected to change incorrect guesses to correct answers, and if you make it clear they will not move forward in the activity until they have some guesses, they will put something down. Once they have a prediction, human nature kicks in and they are eager to see how they did. Think about the science units you teach and the science activities your students engage in and you will quickly envision many prediction think-write possibilities.

> Which objects will sink and which will float?

> Will more water in the glass make the pitch higher or lower?

> When we roll all these round objects down the ramp, which one will hit the ground first?

> Today, we are going to test clay soil, loamy soil, sand, and pebbles to see how quickly water flows through them and how much water is absorbed. Take a piece of scratch paper and order these four from slowest movement to quickest movement. Then order them from absorbs most water to absorbs least water.

In math, we also want students to learn to predict—these predictions are referred to as *estimates*. Teachers often ask their students to give oral estimates before doing math activities. Having the students write their predictions on scratch paper increases the participation and engagement for all students.

> Today, we are going to continue working on two-digit multiplication. I'm going to tell you some numbers you are soon going to multiply and I want you to guess to the nearest hundred what the correct answer will be. Your number must be 100, 200, 300, etc. I have five problems I want you to estimate, so number your scratch paper from 1 to 5.

> We are continuing to work with measurement today and we are going to measure and compute some areas and perimeters. We'll use our metric rulers, so our answers will be in centimeters. As I show you each object you are going to measure, write down the name of the object and your guess of the perimeter and area of that object, making sure your guess is in centimeters.

Prediction think-writes also work well in social studies, although they take a very different form from those done in science classrooms. Informational pieces often have lots of graphics—photos, illustrations, maps, charts, graphs, and others. Students need to learn to use the graphics—and accompanying labels, captions, and other short text—to stimulate their brains to access and build prior knowledge. The prediction think-write you may use to help students learn to "mine" the graphics is very similar to that used in the two-minute think-write you use to help students access prior knowledge. Instead of two minutes, we give them three minutes. Imagine that you are about to read a piece on Ecuador in your *Time for Kids, Scholastic,* or *Weekly Reader.*

> We are going to read a short piece about Ecuador today. Before we read, I am going to give you exactly three minutes to "mine" the graphics. Look at all the graphics—photos, illustrations, maps, charts, graphs—anything visual, and write down as many things as you can that you think we are going to learn about Ecuador. You can use the labels, captions, and other short text that go with the graphics but don't waste your three minutes reading the longer pieces of text. Take a piece of scrap paper and get started. You have three minutes to write down as many things as you can about Ecuador. You may start now!

When the three minutes are up, have your students put the text out of sight and ask them to volunteer what they learned about Ecuador from the graphics. Just as in the accessing prior knowledge think-write, you accept their answers and ask expanding or clarifying questions as appropriate.

Yes, Ecuador is on the equator. Does anyone remember what the equator is?

Yes, bananas are a major crop. Do you think they keep all the bananas they grow there or export them?

Right, Ecuador is about the size of Nebraska. Do you think that makes it larger or smaller than our state?

Ecuador
Equator
South America
mountains
borders Peru+
    Colombia
jungle
Pacific Ocean

As your students share information and think about your expansions on their ideas, they are going to want to return to the piece again and point out more information from the graphics. Explain that they will be reading the whole piece soon but until then you want them to focus on how much they were able to glean from the graphics in just three minutes. If you catch someone sneaking a peak, remove the text from that student and return it when it is time to read. Adhere firmly to your "no sneak peaks" rule during the first several three-minute "predict what you will learn" think-writes, knowing that your students will learn to make maximum use of their three minutes in future lessons.

Reading and literature are other areas in which you can do prediction think-writes. When your students are reading informational text during a reading lesson, you can use the "mine the graphics" procedure just described. If your students are going to read a story, you can ask them to write down predictions of what will happen in the story. The first predictions should be based just on the cover and title. Once students have written three predictions, read aloud to them the first several pages and see if any of their predictions based on the title and cover actually happened. Once you have your students successfully launched into the story, ask them to write down three more predictions and then let them finish reading the story to see if any of these predictions actually happened.

Prediction is a powerful motivator that you can use to engage the attention of your students. When you use the prediction think-writes, the brains of more students are more deeply engaged.

Principal will kiss pig
Pig will run away
kids will read 10 000 books

What About My Advanced Writers?

The regular use of a variety of think-writes will engage all your students—regardless of their writing levels. Think-writes require you to give students wait time, which has been shown in numerous studies to raise the level of thinking students do and increase participation.

Think-Writes to Summarize

In addition to helping students make connections and predictions, think-writes can also be used to help your students think and learn by sharpening their ability to determine important information and summarize what they have learned. Let's return to our Ecuador example discussed in the previous section. You gave your students three minutes to mine the graphics and write down what they thought they were going to learn based just on the graphics and accompanying quicktext. Students shared their predictions and you affirmed these and asked clarifying and extending questions. Next, your students will read the text.

Before letting them reopen the text, give each student three sticky notes. Tell them to read all the text and use the sticky notes to mark the three most interesting or important facts they learn about Ecuador. Show them how to write a brief sentence or phrase telling what they think is important and place the sticky note right on the place of the page where they found that information.

The first time you do this with your students, they will probably use their sticky notes quickly and ask for more. Make it clear that there is a lot of information about Ecuador in this short piece and that they can't sticky-note everything. Their job is to choose three interesting facts they want to remember and share. Don't give them any additional sticky notes. Letting them cover the piece with sticky notes would defeat your purpose of helping them learn to think about what information is most interesting and important. You may want to have your students work in partners to read and sticky-note the text, partnering struggling readers with stronger readers who will help them with difficult words.

When students complete the reading, gather them together and go through each part of the text, asking who has a sticky note on this page. Have them read what they wrote on the sticky note and explain why they think this is an interesting or important fact. You can use three sticky note

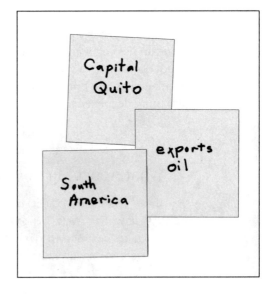

think-writes in any subject area when students are reading informational text and you want them to think about what information is most important or interesting to them.

What If?

What if I Use KWLs to Help Students Connect, Predict, and Summarize?

The think-writes described in this chapter work wonderfully within the framework of a KWL. Before filling in information on the *K* (*Know*) column of the chart, give students two minutes to jot down on scratch paper everything they know. As they share what they know, record this on the chart. If students tell you something incorrect, record that in the *W* (*Want to Learn*) column and indicate you are not sure that is correct and that is one of the questions we will see if we can answer. Record other questions students have also in the Q column. Give students three sticky notes and tell them to use these to mark the three things they want to add to the *L* (*Learned*) column. The think-writes in this chapter work very well without the formal KWL structure but they can also make your KWL more engaging and efficient.

To conclude a unit or topic, you may want students to summarize the important information they have learned. To do this, you can ask them to write a paragraph and give them a paragraph starter. For Ecuador, you might ask them to begin their paragraph with:

I have learned many interesting facts about Ecuador.

After doing an experiment in science with objects that sink and float, you might ask them to summarize what they have learned with a paragraph starter such as:

When you put them in water, some things sink and some things float.

Give your students a short time—five to eight minutes—to complete this summary think-write and then let volunteers share what they wrote. If you have your

> Ecuador
> I have learned many
> interesting facts about
> Ecuador. Ecuador is a medium
> size country in South America.
> It borders Peru and Colombia.
> The Andes mountains and the
> Galapagos islands are in
> Ecuador. The Galapagos giant
> tortoise can way 500 pounds.
> Ecuador exports bananas and
> oil. Children in Ecuador play
> soccer and like TV and movies.

> When you put them in water, some
> things sink and some things float.
> Apples bananas pencils and blocks
> float. keys rocks and crayons sink.
> Things float if they dont way much
> for there size. They sink if
> they way alot.

students keep learning logs or subject-specific notebooks, you may want them to write their summary think-writes in these logs or notebooks. Another possibility is to give them a large index card and have them write their summary on it.

Pick Up Your Thinking Pens
(instead of "Put on your thinking caps")

Have you ever told your students to "put on their thinking caps"? What does that mean? Most of us use that expression but what sense do our students make of that? Instead of telling your students to put on their thinking caps, you may want to tell them to "Pick up your thinking pens." Having specific pens that students write with when they are doing a think-write helps your students keep the purpose of think-writes clearly in mind. The purpose of the writing you are asking them to do is to help them think.

If the thinking pen idea appeals to you, have these pens readily available with your supply of scratch paper and don't allow your students to use them except when they are doing think-writes. This makes the thinking pens—as well as the think-writes—special! Students particularly like using the thinking pens if you provide them in a color—purple, pink, or green—not normally used in the classroom. Thinking pens are not essential to think-writes but they do clearly signal to the students when the writing you are asking them to do is different from a lot of the writing they do in your classroom. We use the thinking pens when we are writing for ourselves—to help us think about what we know, predict what we will learn, decide what we think is important, and summarize what we have learned.

When you are making a list or writing a reminder to yourself, you don't think about the fact that you are writing. Similarly, your students won't bring their negative writing attitudes with them to think-writes. Think-writes are a different kind of writing—on a different kind of paper and in some classrooms with a different kind of pen. Think-writes are never long and the teacher is always focused on the good ideas the students are sharing, not the correctness of the writing. Think-writes are single-draft writing that do not need to be edited because this writing, unlike other writing, is not for other people to read.

When you incorporate think-writes into your day, an increased amount of thinking will be done by more of your students. If a greater number of students are thinking more, they will also be learning more. The other benefit of including think-writes in all areas of your curriculum throughout the school day is that your students will be writing more. We talked in the first chapter about the reluctance of many students to write and their tendency to write only as much as they have to. "How many sentences do I have to write?" is a question commonly heard in elementary classrooms. To become better writers, students need instruction and lots of practice. Think-writes are a "sneaky" way of providing your students with extra writing practice. Because the purpose of think-writes is to get students to think, they do not need to be revised.

Looking Back
Think-Writes across the Curriculum

Incorporate think-writes throughout your school day:

- Use two-minute, scratch-paper think-writes to activate prior knowledge.
- Have students write down predictions (guesses) and then check these out as they read.
- Give students three sticky notes on which to note the three most interesting or important facts they are learning from a piece of informational text.
- Have students write and share short summaries written on index cards or in their subject-specific notebooks.
- Consider using some special thinking pens to distinguish think-writes from other kinds of writing.

Chapter 5

Editing Matters!

As with spelling, student writers are expected to grow in their ability to comply with the conventions of writing mechanics and language usage as they move up through the grades.

The mechanics of writing are capitalization, punctuation, and formatting (name and date on the paper, good margins, title centered, etc.). Language usage includes such additional conventions as having complete sentences and avoiding double negatives. You must read a paper to find errors in spelling and mechanics, but you can find errors in usage whether you read the paper or someone reads it to you. The ideas and content of writing are more important than spelling, mechanics, and usage, but students are reluctant to write—and others are reluctant to read what they've written—when their writing is filled with errors.

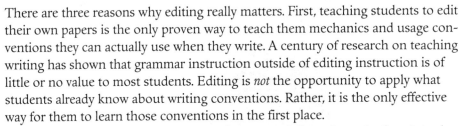 Why Editing Really Matters

There are three reasons why editing really matters. First, teaching students to edit their own papers is the only proven way to teach them mechanics and usage conventions they can actually use when they write. A century of research on teaching writing has shown that grammar instruction outside of editing instruction is of little or no value to most students. Editing is *not* the opportunity to apply what students already know about writing conventions. Rather, it is the only effective way for them to learn those conventions in the first place.

The second reason why editing really matters follows from the first. It is also important to teach students to edit their own papers so they will learn the essential writing strategies of proofreading and self-correction. It is these two strategies that will enable your students to become independent in producing more correct papers, and to learn the writing rules you teach them. Many students can quote writing rules and complete worksheets on those rules, but they can't proofread and correct their own papers for those rules. If you look at the writing they produce, it appears they don't know the rules. The first reason to teach students to edit was that most of them will only really learn writing and language conventions by learning how to edit their own papers. However, children can't learn conventions during editing unless they know how to edit! In other words, children should begin learning to edit their own papers soon after the first writing rules have been introduced to them, usually by the middle of first grade. Until they learn to edit their own papers for one or two simple writing rules, they won't be able to use editing to learn more complex rules. When students begin learning how to edit their own writing using a few simple conventions, they are simultaneously beginning to learn the essential writing strategies of proofreading and self-correction. If students consistently have many errors in spelling, mechanics, and usage in their writing, they need to begin to learn how to proofread and self-correct for just a few conventions.

The third reason why editing really matters is that it provides students with an incentive to write correctly during their first drafts without penalizing them when they are unable to do so. During first-draft writing, students are simultaneously trying to spell words correctly, follow mechanics and usage conventions, and turn their thoughts into words! So, a separate editing step in the writing process—during which writers are focused solely on finding and fixing some of their spelling, mechanical, and usage errors—helps them produce final drafts with fewer errors than their first drafts. Just as importantly, however, a separate editing step also provides your students with an incentive to do things right to start with, on first drafts, if they can, since it is less work for a writer to do that than later to have to find and fix the errors during editing. Teaching editing makes it clear to everyone that correctness is important, and holds students accountable for an appropriate degree of correctness in their final drafts, without causing the discouragement that grading first drafts for correctness inevitably does.

It is this third reason for teaching editing that is most responsible for students making progress in the mechanics and usage conventions they can apply during first-draft writing. Students who do not know a convention well enough to follow it consistently during first-draft writing learn to find and fix their errors on that convention during the editing step. As they repeatedly discover and correct their errors during editing, you will see them gradually make fewer errors on that convention in their first drafts. Eventually, they will not need to edit for that convention anymore and will be ready to learn to edit their papers for another convention. Older students who still do not consistently start sentences with capital letters or end them with appropriate ending punctuation in their first drafts are revealing that they have not had enough instruction and practice editing their first drafts for those particular rules.

What If?

What if My School Teaches Mechanics and Grammar the Old-Fashioned Way?

Unfortunately, the traditional way of teaching students to follow the conventions of mechanics and usage when they write doesn't work very well. Why? Because it relies on teaching students jargon and rules rather than teaching them to apply conventions in their own writing. In traditional grammar instruction, students are taught to identify the names of parts of speech, and sometimes even the names of parts of sentences (subject, predicate, direct object, etc.). They are also taught to remember rules such as capitalize proper nouns, end sentences with appropriate punctuation, indent each new paragraph, maintain subject-verb agreement, and many others.

(continued)

This traditional way of teaching mechanics and usage conventions is significantly different from best practices in teaching decoding, spelling, computation, swimming, playing the piano, and a host of other skills both in and outside of school. In all these other cases, we minimize jargon and rules, only introducing them when they seem useful as we coach students how to do the skill we are teaching them. For example, an extended period of time spent teaching children to identify which letters are consonants, which are vowels, and which are blends, diphthongs, digraphs, or silent before trying to teach them to decode three- or four-letter words would surely be ineffective. Likewise with computation in mathematics. We have never seen a teacher teach students the jargon and rules of computation, for an extended period, without trying to teach them to add, subtract, multiply, or divide! Unfortunately, we have seen teachers teaching parts of speech and rules for mechanics and usage with little or no time spent on teaching the students how to actually write with correct mechanics and usage! It is a mystery to us why students are taught so much jargon and rules when no research supports the traditional grammar method of teaching mechanics and usage for writing.

How to Begin

In Chapter 1, we described how each school year should begin with writing instruction that helps students see writing as a way to "tell" and share their experiences and ideas. Only when most of the children are writing fluently and willingly—if not well—is it time to teach them how to edit their writing. Depending on the age of the students and their previous experiences (both positive and negative) with writing, the focus on editing might begin a few weeks or a few months into the school year.

Most writers don't like to edit (present company included!). Editing implies you "messed up" the first time. Why else would you have to go back and "fix it"? Many children think that they are the only ones who have to edit or fix errors in their writing. The first thing your students need to understand is that all writing—even that of the most famous writers—needs editing. Of course, you can tell your students that all writers—even the very best—edit their own writing and then have professional editors edit it again before it is published. But how much more powerful this message will be when you show them!

Mini-lessons are the first and most frequent means of getting this important message across. Before asking your students to edit their own papers the first time, it is vital that you have taught them how to help you edit your writing. Since you automatically comply with the conventions you are teaching them, you may need to explain to them that you are making errors on purpose so they can help you find them, because that is what you will soon be teaching them to do in their own writing. As we explained earlier, some teachers use mini-lessons to show their students "how I wrote when I was your age."

It also really helps students understand the need and value of editing if you bring a real "published" writer into your classroom and ask that writer to bring some of his or her "before and after" writing. At this point, you may be thinking that you don't know any writers—but that isn't likely to be true. Perhaps you don't know any famous writers but what about people who write pieces for your local newspaper? Newspapers are usually very willing to support school literacy programs, counting on you to produce their next generation of readers. They might even be willing to send one of their writers and one of their editors to talk to your class, especially if you gather the whole grade level or school together and make it a big event. Wouldn't some of your children love to meet the person who writes the local sports column and the editor who does the final edit? Another possibility is to invite the editor of the high school newspaper to your class one day. Or, how about a local church or community group that publishes a weekly or monthly newsletter? All those pieces were written—and usually edited—before they were published. Our guess is that all teachers know someone who is a "published author" (or know someone who knows a published author). If you can arrange for a writer and/or an editor to "show and tell" with your children, you can forevermore banish the idea that editing your writing is just what kids have to do because they aren't good writers yet.

However you accomplish this important goal, your children's attitudes toward editing will improve immensely if you can convince them that all—even the very best and most famous writers—edit their own writing and then have professional editors do a final edit before publishing.

The First Editing Mini-Lessons

When you begin to teach your students to edit, focus first on something simple that you think will make the biggest difference in the writing of most of your students. Remember that what they are really learning first is *how to proofread and self-correct their own papers*. The specific conventions they edit for at first help them learn these two essential strategies when they are relatively easy to find and fix. Also, simple beginnings will bring about early success, therefore your students will be willing to edit in the future as you gradually introduce more writing rules.

The first editing lesson you teach is very important because it will shape your students' attitude toward editing. Imagine that you are about to teach the first editing lesson in your classroom. You want students to begin to learn to proofread and edit by checking to see that all their sentences made sense. Here is what your first editing mini-lessons might look like and sound like.

Your students are used to your sitting down at the overhead or computer and writing something each day at the beginning of writing time. They know that you write what you want to tell them and that some days you don't finish your piece and will reread it and add on to it the next day. They also expect that you will use the word wall, monthly chart, and other print in the room to support spelling, and that you will stretch out and circle a few words you can spell now but couldn't spell when you were their age. Before you begin to write today, you tell them that they will begin learning to do something new this week. They are all going to learn to become editors!

Boys and girls, who remembers when Mr. Marr from the *Daily Sun* came to visit our school last week? Do you remember what his job is at the paper? Yes, he is the sports editor. He writes some of the sports articles and he edits all the articles written by other writers. Who remembers what an editor does? Yes, an editor fixes any errors and makes sure the piece is easy for people to read. Everything you read—books, magazines, newspapers—has a writer and an editor. Even famous writers need editors because writing is complex and no one is perfect. We are going to start choosing some of our best pieces to publish soon and they will need to be edited. Starting today, I am going to teach you all how to be editors so you can edit your own writing and help your friends edit their writing.

When editors edit writing, they sometimes have a checklist. We are going to have a checklist for editing our writing. Here is the beginning of our checklist with just one item we need to edit for.

Editor's Checklist

1. Do all the sentences make sense?

Who can read the question next to number 1? Yes, one very important thing editors always check is to make sure that all the sentences make sense. Sometimes, writers leave out words or forget to finish a sentence and then the sentences don't make sense. Today, when I am writing, I am going to write one sentence that doesn't make sense. Please don't interrupt my thinking by telling me as soon as I write it. When I finish my writing for the day, we will read my sentences together and then you can tell me which sentence does not make sense and help me fix it.

Next, write your piece as you always do except purposely leave out a word. Your students who are, as always, reading along as you write will notice your mistake immediately, but you just keep writing, giving them the look that says, "Don't interrupt my thinking!" When you finish writing, you say:

Now let's read my piece together and see if all my sentences make sense. Give me a "thumbs up" if the sentence makes sense.

The students and you read one sentence at a time and they indicate with a "thumbs up" that the sentences thus far have made sense. When you get to the sentence where you left out a word, the students are quick to give you a "thumbs down."

You're right. This sentence doesn't make sense because my mind got ahead of my marker. Let me show you how editors fix a sentence with a missing word. They put a ^ where the word should have gone and then insert the word above the line over the ^.

You and your students continue to read the remaining sentences, all of which get a "thumbs up" for making sense. You thank them for their editing help and the students go off to their own writing. When the writing time is up, you quickly pass out red pens to your students as you point to the *editor's checklist* and say:

Be your own editor now. Read your paper and see if all your sentences make sense. Give yourself a thumbs up if the sentence makes sense. If you find a sentence that doesn't make sense, give yourself a thumbs down and use this red editor's pen to fix that sentence.

You watch as the children do their best to see if their sentences made sense and notice a few children writing something with their red pens. After just a minute, say:

Good. Now, use your red pen to draw yourself a little happy face to show you checked your sentences for making sense. Put your red pen back in this container as it is passed to you. We will need them again tomorrow when we practice being editors.

Every day, for the next week or two, when you write, you should include one sentence that does not make sense. Sometimes, you leave a word out or don't finish a sentence. Some days, you write a similar word—*were* for *where, how* for *who*. The children will delight in being your editor and catching your mistake. Each day, show them how an editor fixes that error and makes the sentence make sense.

When the allotted writing time is up each day, you quickly hand out red pens. The children read their sentences, giving themselves a thumbs up or thumbs down for each and occasionally fixing a mistake. They don't find every problem but they all know what they are trying to do and the physical thumbs up/thumbs down signal along with the red pen makes editing an activity they look forward to! Each editing session ends with all the children drawing smiley faces, which means they checked their sentences for making sense. This means every child gets to use the cherished red pens, even if they have no errors in sense making or don't find the ones they do have!

What If?

What if My Students Think All Their Sentences Make Sense?

"Do all the sentences make sense?" is a good writing rule to teach students early in their development as editors because young or struggling writers can understand it without knowing anything about grammar or the jargon of writing. Your students, like the rest of us, however, will not always recognize when a sentence does not make sense. As you teach your students to edit for this and other rules, you need to develop a tolerance for imperfection. Your goal is to help your students learn how to edit their writing and what to edit it for. If most of your students can detect the obvious "not making sense" errors in your writing and in their own, don't worry about the more complex ways in which a sentence does not quite work.

It is also important not to broaden this rule to mean that a sentence has to be nearly perfect mechanically to "make sense." We have seen children have trouble with beginning editing instruction because this rule was taught to them as if it meant "Are all my sentences complete sentences?" and/or "Do all my sentences start with capitals and have ending punc?" Be patient. You will get to the issues complete sentences and appropriate punctuation as the year goes on. The example sentences here make sense. If you see sentences like this in the writing of your students, you will know that complete sentences, beginning capitals, and ending punctuation are items you need to gradually add to your checklist.

- I'm the best skateboarder on my block if you don't think so come to my house and I show you
- Chocolate fudge is the best. Rich. gooey. Sweet. Yummy in the tummy.

After a few weeks, when the children are automatically editing their papers for one thing each day, you then add a second item to the checklist.

Editor's Checklist

1. Do all the sentences make sense?

2. Do all the sentences have ending punc?

Boys and girls, who has noticed something new on our editor's checklist? Yes, you are doing so well with editing for item number 1 that I have added a second item all editors check for. Who can read number 2? Good. You probably figured out that "punc" is an abbreviation for punctuation. Every sentence needs a punctuation mark—a period, a question mark, or an exclamation point—at the end. Today, you will need very sharp eyes to be my editor. I am going to make two mistakes in two different sentences. One of my sentences is not going to make sense and I'm going to forget to put a "punc" mark on another. See if you can catch my mistake. Remember, I don't like it when you interrupt my thinking. Editors do their editing after the writer is finished—not when the writer is in the middle of writing!

You now write something and, as promised, write one sentence that doesn't make sense and leave out the punctuation at the end of another.

This summer my grandson will be one year old! My husband and I are going to go on vacation with him and his parents for a week I can't wait! He will probably be a little strange at first because he hasn't seen. Hopefully, by the end of the week he will know who his grandpa and gram are.

When you and your students read your writing, each sentence is only read once—but the students give you a thumbs up or thumbs down for sense (#1) and for ending punctuation (#2). You fix the errors—adding a period at the end of the second sentence and inserting the words you left out in the fourth sentence. You thank them for being such good editors and send them off to their own writing.

This summer my grandson will be one year old! My husband and I are

going to go on vacation with him and his parents for a week. I can't wait!

He will probably be a little strange at first because he hasn't seen. us very often

Hopefully, by the end of the week he will know who his grandpa and

gram are.

When their writing time is up and you are handing out red pens, remind the children that they now have two things to think about as they read each sentence: Does the sentence make sense and does it have ending punctuation? When they have finished editing, they draw themselves the red smiley face to show they have edited their piece as best they could. Notice in the student example, the child didn't notice that the third sentence doesn't make sense because a word was left out. The child did notice the missing period after *sound* and inserted it. The idea isn't that they edit perfectly but that they get in the habit of checking their writing and they begin to know what to check for.

My cuzin is a pilot
in the air force. She
is in Afganistan. She
went Christmas. Her
airplane goes faster
than sound. Radar
cant see it. We pray
she wont get shot down.

When you begin teaching mini-lessons on proofreading and editing, start reminding your students to skip every other line whenever they write a first draft. Once they begin editing, having a blank line above to insert punctuation, words they forgot to write, and correct spellings makes their edited first drafts much easier for them and you to read. They can put a ∧ where they left out a word or a punctuation mark and write the word or mark in the blank line above the ∧, so they don't have to try to squeeze it in where there's not enough room. In the case of a misspelled word, they just cross it out and write the correct spelling in the blank line above it.

What If?
What if My Students Don't Find All Their Errors?

The biggest concern we have heard teachers voice about having children self-edit for the items on the checklist is, "My students don't find all their errors," to which we respond, "Neither do real writers!" Pat and Jim each edited their own chapters as they wrote this book and then they edited each other's chapters. Both found things that needed editing that the original writer hadn't found. When the book was finally finished and sent off to our publisher, Allyn & Bacon, they edited it and, believe it or not, their professional editor found many more things that needed fixing! When you tell your students, "Be your own editor. Read your piece and give yourself a thumbs-up if your sentence makes sense and another one if it begins with a capital letter," you aren't expecting them to find every sentence that doesn't make sense. Some sentences will sound just right and be perfectly sensible to them but you may need to fix these sentences later as their final editor, if they choose to publish this piece. As published writers, we all too often get back a book with some sentences marked as "doesn't make sense." "But of course it makes sense," we would like to respond, but we know that if it didn't make sense to our editor, it probably won't make sense to our readers. So we say it differently and hope it makes more sense the second time around.

In fact, this tolerance for imperfection in students' writing is a necessary instructional principle when teaching editing as part of the writing process. In addition to the mini-lessons we teach when the class helps us edit what we have written, it is important for us to meet with students, individually or in small groups, who are still having trouble finding and fixing their own errors on the Editor's Checklist. And it is important for us to serve as the final editor for our students, fixing errors for them that they are not yet ready to learn how to fix themselves. However, there is a temptation when we do these things that we need to resist: Sometimes a teacher is tempted to think that the indicator of students' progress in writing is that their final or published drafts are free of mechanical errors. The problem is that, when a goal

(continued)

of writing instruction is to produce an error-free final draft, it can lead teachers to edit *for* children, rather than requiring them to edit their own papers and then checking their editing and fixing a few additional things for them. If we provide too much "help" to our students in editing their papers, it isn't actually helpful to them. They may have more correct final drafts, but they are making less progress in learning how to write correctly because they are not learning to edit their own papers.

Build Your Editor's Checklist Gradually

Walk into a classroom while children are writing and observe the conventions they have control of as they write first drafts. Do most of the children demonstrate that beginning capitalization and ending punctuation are automatic whenever they write? The items on the editor's checklist aren't there just so the children will find them as they edit. The goal is that by focusing on the checklist items as the children check the teacher's writing at the end of mini-lessons and by asking the children to do a quick self-edit of their own writing each day, your students will begin to incorporate these conventions as they write their first drafts. The question of when to add another item to the checklist can be answered by observing the first draft writing of your students. If the majority of your students apply the current checklist items most of the time as they write their first drafts, it is time to add another item to the checklist. If you add additional conventions before most students can do the current ones, many students won't become automatic at any mechanics or usage conventions.

The concept of automaticity is important to all learning but it has a huge effect on how well children write. The brain can do many automatic things—but only *one* nonautomatic thing at a time. Automatic means just what you would think it means—you do it without thinking. The way you become automatic at something is to do it over and over. As students begin each school year, we delay concerns with mechanics and usage conventions and try to get them to write willingly every day. We first want them to become automatic at putting down what they want to tell. We want them to use the word wall and other room supports for spelling and to automatically stretch out other words, putting down the sounds they hear. Whatever punctuation and other conventions they use as they write will be things they have become automatic at through previous writing or because that is the way they have learned to speak at home.

As we watch students write during the first weeks of school, we observe those things that they already do automatically, and these observations inform us about what to add to the editor's checklist. Most first-graders have little automaticity with conventions and we observe that we need to start with the most basic conventions and spend quite a lot of time on each so that they become automatic. If older children have done a lot of writing in previous grades and learned to apply conventions in their own writing, we can combine things on our checklists and just spend a few weeks on those conventions that come automatically for most of the children. Developing your own editor's checklist is easy if you let your observations of your children's first-draft writing determine what is added, the order in which items are added, and the speed with which they are added. If you teach in second or third grade or if you teach students who have not been taught editing well in previous grades, here are some questions to ask yourself as you observe your students' first draft writing early in the year:

- Do most of the sentences make sense?
- Do most sentences begin with capital letters?
- Does *I* have a capital letter?
- Is there ending punctuation at the end of most sentences?
- Is the ending punctuation appropriate to the sentence?
- Do children automatically circle words they stretched out to spell?
- Do most sentences stay on the topic?
- Do people and place names have capital letters?

For older students who automatically do most of these conventions in their first drafts, ask yourself these questions:

- Are paragraphs "real paragraphs" and indented correctly?
- Is dialogue appropriately punctuated?
- Are commas used appropriately?
- Does most writing contain appropriate standard English usage?

Answering these questions can help you see what mechanics and usage conventions to gradually add to the editor's checklist in your classroom.

Teaching the Editor's Checklist Items

Once you have decided what items to add to the editor's checklist and in what order, teaching the items is straightforward. This chapter began with a description of how you might began your editor's checklist and teach your students to read your sentences and their own sentences, thinking about whether or not each made sense. When most students understood what they were editing for and when most of the sentences in their first drafts made sense, another item was added: Do all the sentences have ending punctuation? When most of your students are putting some punctuation at the end of most of their sentences most of the time, you are ready to add item 3 to your list. Don't wait for perfection, however. Some children will think their sentence ends before it does and put the punc mark there. Sometimes, they will put a period when a question mark is needed. What you are looking for is the understanding that sentences need ending punc and that your students are becoming automatic at following this convention most of the time.

When you add item 3, be sure that you continue on some days to make a number 1 or number 2 error. (Don't, however, make too many errors and make your piece unreadable.) As the children write, ask them to read their sentences for all three things. That doesn't mean, however, that they read their sentences three times. Imagine that the third item that you add is: Do all the sentences begin with capitals?

Editor's Checklist

1. Do all the sentences make sense?

2. Do all the sentences have ending punc?

3. Do all the sentences begin with capitals?

As the students read your piece, a sentence at a time, you should ask:

"Make sense?" (Thumbs are all up.)

"Ending punc?" (Thumbs down—add the appropriate punc.)

"Next word has a 'cap'?" (Thumbs up.)

Reading what you write each day for these three basic sentence conventions shouldn't take more than a minute, as should reading their own daily writing for sense, ending punc, and beginning caps.

As the year goes on and your students develop automaticity with each convention, you can add another rule to the checklist. Be careful, however, not to add too many rules too quickly. Remember that you are not just teaching them to edit for these conventions, you are using the editing mini-lessons and self-editing to help them learn to apply the conventions as they write their first drafts. Expect your students to progress from not using the convention in their writing, to noticing when you don't use it correctly, to noticing when they haven't used it correctly as they edit, to using the convention correctly in their writing most of the time. As you teach editing and mechanics, think about how you would learn to juggle. If you start trying to juggle five objects, you will probably drop them all and quickly decide that juggling is just not in your genes! But if you get good at juggling two, and then three, and then four, you may very well discover that you can indeed juggle those five objects.

Teach Children to Peer Edit

Once your students have had lots of experience editing your piece of writing every day, they are ready to learn how to edit with a partner. Most teachers introduce this by choosing one student to be their partner and role-playing how the partner will help with the editing.

> Boys and girls, we are going to pretend today that I am one of the students in this class and I am getting ready to publish a piece and I will choose one of you to be my editor. After I write my piece, instead of letting the whole class read the sentences aloud and do thumbs up or thumbs down as we have been doing, I will choose one of you to be my editor.

You then write your piece, hand one child a marker, and say:

> You are going to be my editor. You and I will read each sentence together and edit for the things on the checklist. There are currently four things on the checklist. As we read each sentence, we will decide if it makes sense and stays on topic, if it has appropriate ending punc, and if first words, I, people, and place names have caps. Then we will look at the words and decide if any of them need to be circled because we think they aren't spelled correctly.

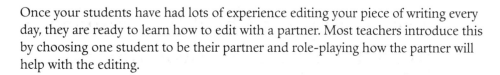

When it rained so hard last (Wendsday,) it flooded my basement. By the time I got home, the water was a couple of feet deep so it was too late to save most of the things I had down there. My neighbor, **J**ay, had a pump he let me borrow so I could pump out all the water. It left a mess! My **W**ashing **M**achine doesn't work anymore.

For the next several days, follow the procedure of choosing one student—a different student each day—to be your editor. Read and edit the piece together as the rest of the students watch. When you think most students understand how to help each other edit for the items on the checklist, partner them up, assigning partners of similar writing ability to work together. Have each child choose a piece and then work with the partner to edit it. Circulate and make sure everyone understands that both partners are to read each sentence for the four things on the checklist and jointly decide what needs fixing. Depending on how successfully they do this, you may have several more peer editing practice sessions before turning the kids loose to peer edit without your supervision.

How the Editor's Checklist Changes as Students Move Up through the Grades

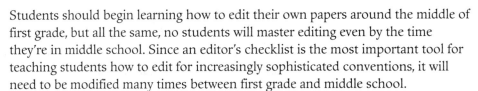

Students should begin learning how to edit their own papers around the middle of first grade, but all the same, no students will master editing even by the time they're in middle school. Since an editor's checklist is the most important tool for teaching students how to edit for increasingly sophisticated conventions, it will need to be modified many times between first grade and middle school.

Whatever grade you teach, when you begin instructing your students how to edit their papers, the editor's checklist should have only one rule on it. As students learn how to find and fix their errors on that rule in their writing, you add a second rule to the checklist. When students are generally successful with those two rules, you add a third. Eventually, the editor's checklist will have five or six rules on it that your students are responsible for complying with in their edited drafts. We have found that having more than five or six rules on the checklist causes many students to tire and give up before they are through editing their first drafts. Consequently, before adding a new rule to the editor's checklist with five or six rules, you should remove one. If you are only adding a new rule when your students are generally using a convention in their first-draft writing, your students should no longer need the first rule to be on the checklist by the time you are ready to add a sixth or seventh one.

A second way that editor's checklists change from grade to grade is whether each rule on the checklist is a single convention or whether two or more conventions have been combined into a single rule. For example, if you notice that most students have ending punctuation at the ends of most sentences but that question marks and exclamation points are rarely or inappropriately used, you may want to have three separate rules on your editor's checklist for ending punctuation:

Do questions end with a question mark?

Do exciting sentences end with an exclamation point?

Do other sentences end with a period?

Adding these three rules, one at a time, to your editor's checklist helps your youngest or most challenged students eventually learn how to have correct punctuation at the end of all their sentences.

However, upper-grade teachers often notice that most of their students follow each of those three rules some of the time but not consistently in their first drafts. In that case, rather than putting these three conventions on their editor's checklist as three rules, they combine the three conventions into one rule and add it to the checklist:

Sentences end with appropriate punctuation.

When students follow each ending punctuation convention some of the time, the conventions can be combined into one rule that still helps these students find and fix the errors they do make in ending punctuation. Combining the three into one leaves room for other rules on the editor's checklist without it becoming too long.

Other rules for upper grades that combine two or more conventions into one rule are:

Sentences make sense and stay on topic.

First word, I, people, and place names have caps.

Commas are used appropriately.

Apostrophes are used appropriately.

Sentences are complete—but not choppy or run-on.

Quotations are punctuated appropriately.

If, on the other hand, a convention is not used by most of your students, you still need to break it out into a separate item on your editor's checklist. New conventions are best learned when students can focus on finding and fixing errors on them one at a time.

What If?

What if Some of My Students Don't Speak Standard English?

Usage conventions, unlike writing mechanics, can apply to both speaking and writing. For example, a double negative can occur as readily in speech as in a first draft. Traditionally, this fact about usage has caused some teachers to try to correct children's speech in order to improve their usage in writing. However, this practice is generally ineffective because it is much easier to learn to correct one's usage while writing than while speaking. Writing sits there on the page and so is available for consideration or re-reading as many times as needed. Speaking flies by and is gone forever, except in the rare cases where it is recorded. In writing, we can teach students to proofread and self-correct their errors on targeted usage conventions, until they make few errors on those conventions in their first drafts. In speech, it is not possible to teach students to "proof-listen" and self-correct their usage errors because what they just said is no longer available for them to work on it! Once students learn not to make a particular usage error in their writing, they are ready to learn not to make it when they talk.

When Your Students Begin to Publish, You Are Their Editor-in-Chief

All published writers edit their own writing, sometimes with the help of friends, in order to eliminate as many of their errors in spelling, mechanics, and usage as they can. Even so, before their writing is published in a book, magazine, or newspaper, a professional editor will work with the author to eliminate remaining errors. That is the process we as authors followed when writing the book you are now reading. When your students begin to publish pieces they have written, you become their "professional" editor—the editor-in-chief of your classroom's "publishing company."

Teaching your students how to edit their own papers, as we have discussed so far in this chapter, doesn't have much to do with being your students' professional

editor whenever they publish a piece. In fact, while you are teaching your students how to proofread and self-correct their own papers for the editor's checklist, it is essential that you avoid editing their papers for them. When you do serve as editor-in-chief on the pieces your students publish, you should find only an occasional error for the items on the editor's checklist, because it was their responsibility to find those errors when they edited their papers. Rather, you are primarily editing for misspelled words *not* on the word wall and errors on conventions *not* on the editor's checklist, because your students aren't ready to find and fix these for themselves.

Before your students begin to publish, they don't need you to give their pieces a final edit; once they begin to publish, you need to give only the pieces they publish a final edit, not everything they write. Before you edit a piece they are going to publish, be sure they have edited it first alone and then with a partner for the rules on the editor's checklist.

What About My Advanced Writers?

The editor's checklist in a classroom consists of the writing conventions you are attempting to teach all your students. Many advanced writers also need this instruction, usually because their knowledge of conventions lags behind their creativity, language, and knowledge of topics to write about. However, some of your students may already conform to almost all of the conventions on your editor's checklist in their first drafts. Your best opportunity for meeting their needs comes in the writing conferences they have with you. In some classrooms, as children develop in their writing, they do some peer revising/editing and then come to the teacher "editor-in-chief" for some final revision/editing before publishing. When teachers help children publish the piece they have chosen, they have the opportunity to truly "individualize" their teaching. Looking at the writing of the child usually reveals both what the child needs to move forward and what the child is ready to understand. The conference provides the "teachable moment" in which both advanced and struggling writers can be nudged forward in their literacy development.

Advanced writers often require less repetition than other students to learn a new convention. Consequently, explaining a convention to them in a conference and then asking them to quickly edit their own paper for that convention while you watch can help them much more than it would a student less advanced in knowledge of conventions and ability to edit.

Looking Back

Editing Matters!

To help your students write better first drafts and edit their own writing:

- Convince your students that even the best writers edit their own writing and have editors do a final edit. Show and Tell with a published author if possible.
- Don't begin editing instruction until your students are writing willingly and fluently—if not well!
- Observe your students' first-draft writing to decide what important mechanics and usage conventions are automatic and what you still need to focus on.
- Remind the students to skip every other line when they are writing any first draft they may later edit.
- Begin your checklist with one writing rule. Let students edit your piece for this one rule every day. When the writing time is up, ask students to edit their writing for the one item on the checklist.
- Add a second item when almost all of your students do the first item correctly in their first drafts most of the time. Continue to add items gradually, using the same procedures to teach each.
- Teach students to peer-edit for the items on the editor's checklist by role-playing and then provide supervised practice as they peer-edit with assigned partners of similar ability.
- When your students are publishing a piece, have them peer-edit their chosen piece for the editor's checklist.
- Put your editor-in-chief hat on and do a final edit. Include conventions not yet on your editor's checklist that are needed to make the writing readable by others.
- Later, after they learn to revise, always have them revise *before* editing so they won't need to edit their paper twice.

Chapter **6**

Writing and Editing across the Curriculum

In Chapter 4, we described a variety of think-writes that you can use across your school day to help students think more, learn more, and write more.

Once you begin teaching your students to edit, you can include some larger pieces of writing. Unlike the think-writes that are single-draft writing and have no need to be edited because they are writing that the students do for themselves, the writing done for others to read will need to be edited. The editing will follow the procedures outlined in the previous chapter. After writing a first draft, students will work with a partner to edit for the items currently on the checklist. The purpose of this partner-editing step is to help students notice and develop automaticity with the editing checklist items. Both the writer and the editing partner will benefit from the increased practice they get by always working together to edit a piece for the items on the checklist.

When the partner editing is complete, you will put on your editor-in-chief hat and do a final edit. The goal here is to make the piece readable and acceptable to the people who will be reading the piece. Misspelled words are corrected. Mechanical and usage errors, including punctuation, capitalization, and standard written English conventions, are fixed—even those that are not yet on the checklist. After the piece has been partner-edited and edited by the editor-in-chief, the writer produces a final draft that (hopefully!) incorporates all the editing.

The pieces of writing described in this chapter are short pieces—not as short as think-writes, but not long extended pieces like those described in Chapter 8. All these pieces are connected to the content of what is being studied, and the knowledge needed to achieve the writing is being built as part of the science, social studies, math, or literature unit. There are numerous opportunities for students to produce short, edited pieces as they study various topics across the school year. In this chapter, we will describe some popular writing forms that can be adapted to many subject areas and used at different grade levels.

Cinquain Poems

Imagine that your class is finishing a unit on weather. You have observed weather on various days. You have read several books about weather and have used the Internet to take virtual fieldtrips to places that have weather your area rarely experiences. You have collected weather words and these are displayed along with weather pictures on a weather bulletin board. You decide to have all your students write a short piece about weather and to publish these in a class book. You could have them write in any number of ways but you decide that weather is a good topic for cinquain poetry. Here is the lesson you might teach to enable all your students to write, edit, and publish a cinquain poem on weather.

Boys and girls, this week you are all going to be poets! You are all going to write a poem about weather and we are going to publish them in a class book like this one my last year's class wrote about animals. The special kind of poetry we are going to use is called cinquain poetry. Let me read several of the poems last year's poets wrote and see if you can figure out what makes a poem a cinquain poem.

Rattlesnakes

Poisonous   creatures

Slithering,   hissing,   attacking

Kills   prey   with   venom

Reptiles

Salamanders

Insect   eaters

Swimming,   crawling,   hunting

Like   cool,   damp   places

Amphibians

Grasshoppers

Plant   eaters

Hopping,   jumpling,   leaping

Live   only   one   year

Insects

After reading the poems to your students, help them determine the form. A cinquain poem has five lines. The first line has one word and is the title, the second line has two words, the third line has three words, and the fourth has four words. The last line has one word that is either the same word as the title or a synonym for the title. The type of words that go on each line can vary depending on your topic.

Our cinquains are all going to be about different types of weather. Let's look at the words and pictures on our Weather Board. Who can tell me some types of weather we have learned about? Yes, we have learned about rain and sun and hurricanes and tornadoes and blizzards and thunderstorms and many other kinds of weather. I am going to pick one kind of weather to write about. Make a guess in your mind about what kind of weather I will pick. I will write the type of weather here on this first line. I can tell by your reaction that some of you guessed thunderstorms and you were right. The title of my cinquain is *Thunderstorms* and I have written it on this first line.

Thunderstorms

For the second line, I need two words and I want two describing words—two words that describe thunderstorms. What are some words you can think of that describe thunderstorms?

Your students suggest describing words—*loud, scary, dark, powerful, frightening*—and you choose two to write on line 2.

Thunderstorms

loud, scary

On the third line, I want to use three words that end in *-ing* that tell what happens in a thunderstorm. There are lots of words I could use, but I think I will use these three.

Thunderstorms

loud, scary

Raining, lightning, thundering

The fourth line is going to be a phrase that has four words. Help me think of some good four-word phrases that tell about thunderstorms. I will write them down and then I will choose one.

Your students will suggest several, which you write down and then select one to write on line four.

Thunderstorms

loud, scary

Raining, lightning, thundering

Thunder follows the lightning

Who remembers what we put on the last line? Yes, we either repeat the title or we put another word that means almost the same. I think I will repeat the title and see how it sounds.

Thunderstorms

loud, scary

Raining, lightning, thundering

Thunder follows the lightning

Thunderstorms

You and your students read the cinquain together and decide it sounds good and you are happy with it. The lesson continues:

Now, you are going to write your cinquain. I have made some copies that show you the form that will help you get the right number of words on each line. When you get the paper, count the lines on each line and notice the punctuation I put there.

_____

_____ , _____

_____ , _____ , _____

_____ _____ _____ _____

_____

What do you notice about the lines? Yes, there is just one line for the first line. What will you write on that line? Right, your title will go there—one word that tells the type of weather you will write about. What do you notice about the second line? Yes, there are two lines for words and I put the comma there to separate the words. What kinds of words are you going to write on line 2? Right, describing words. On line 3, there are three lines for three words separated by commas. What kind of words will you use? Right, three words that end in *-ing* and tell something your weather does. And what goes on the last line? Exactly! The same word as the title or a word that means about the same thing.

Now you can write about any kind of weather you choose—except thunderstorms. Turn to your planning partner and talk about which type of weather you will write about. When you each have decided on your weather, put your hands on your head so I will know you are ready.

When most hands are on heads, you let several of your students tell what weather they plan to write about.

Good, we will have cinquains about many types of weather. Now, look at my cinquain and tell me what kind of words you will put on line 2. Yes, describing words. Talk with your partner about some good words that describe your weather.

You continue in this fashion, using your model to remind students about what type of words you used for each line of your cinquain and letting them talk with their partners for just a minute about possibilities for that line. You circulate among the students and help them brainstorm ideas if they need that help.

OK. I think you are ready to write your cinquain. Just as we always do, use the room to help you spell—especially the words on the Weather Board. Stretch out any words you are not sure how to spell and circle them so your editing partner and I can help you fix them.

Your students begin to write. You circulate and do some individual coaching as needed on the type of word for each line. Perhaps you will spot a child trying to write five words on line 4, such as:

Rain makes the plants grow

Help that child eliminate one word and change it to:

Rain makes plants grow

For the following day's mini-lesson, you lead the students to edit your piece, including some specific conventions for cinquain poetry.

Boys and girls, we are going to edit our cinquains. We will use the editor's checklist but we will need to change it a little because a cinquain is a special type of writing.

Editor's Checklist

1. Do all the sentences make sense?

2. Do all the sentences have ending punc?

3. Do all the sentences start with capitals?

4. Are misspelled words circled?

We don't have to check for numbers 1 and 2 because we don't have sentences and so we don't need any ending punc. Even thought we don't have sentences, we do need to check for number 3 because the first word on every line of a poem needs a capital and of course we need to check to make sure we have circled words we think are not spelled correctly. Let's look at my piece and check for number 3 and number 4

Thunderstorms

loud, scary

Raining, lightning, thundering

Thunder follows the lightning

Thunderstorms

The students read your piece and decide that you need a capital *L* on *loud* because *loud* is the first word on that line. You fix the *l* and thank them for their help.

One more special thing we need to check for is that we have the right number and kind of words on each line. When you are editing with your partner, I want you to use my cinquain as a model and make sure you have the title on line one, two describing words on line 2, three -ing words on line 3, a four-word phrase on line 4, and the title again or a synonym on the last line.

So you are checking for three things: number 3 and number 4 on our checklist and the right number and kind of words on each line. Get a red pen and go with your editing partner and begin editing. When you have edited together, bring your cinquain to me for a final edit.

Your students will edit together as best they can. They then line up for your final edit. You fix some spellings and help a few of them adjust the number of words on each line. Your children then copy and illustrate their cinquain on the class book page that you have designed. The bottom half of the page contains the form including lines and commas and a place for the poet's name. The top half is where they will illustrate their poems.

Important Poems

Another poetry format that students enjoy writing and that works well in many different subject areas is the Important Poem based on *The Important Book* by Margaret Wise Brown. Begin your instruction by reading this book aloud to your students. After enjoying the book, return to the pages and notice the pattern. The first sentence sets up the topic and tells the most important thing about it. The next sentences tell more facts about the topic. The last sentence repeats the first sentence. You could use this poem format to write about many topics you study in your classroom. Imagine that you have been reading biographies of famous Americans—including the engaging picture book biographies written by David Adler. You decide that the Important Poem format is a good way for your students to share what they learned in researching a famous American. You choose Amelia Earhart as the subject of your important poem and, with the students watching, you reread the biography of Amelia Earhart and complete a web as a planning device.

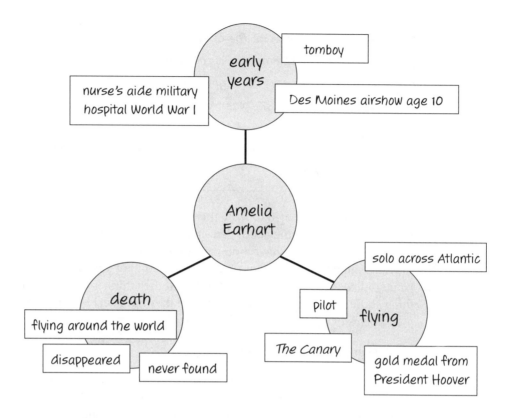

Next, your students then choose *their* famous Americans and, using whatever sources they have, construct webs of information they want to include.

On the following day, your students watch as you use the information on your web to help you compose this Amelia Earhart poem.

Amelia Earhart

The important thing about Amelia Earhart is that she was a courageous woman.

When she was growing up, everyone called her a tomboy.

She was a nurse's aide in a military hospital during the first world war.

She saw her first airplane at the Des Moines airshow when she was 10 years old.

She became a pilot and bought an airplane.

She named the airplane *The Canary*.

She was the first woman to fly solo across the atlantic ocean.

President hoover gave her a gold medal.

She disappeared as she was trying to fly around the world.

She was never found.

But the important thing about Amelia Earhart is that she was a courageous woman.

Before students begin to write their poems, ask them to think about what is the most important thing about their famous person. Point out to them that you didn't have the word *courageous* on your web but you decided that her courage was the most important thing about her so you used it for your first and last line. Have your students talk with a partner about what they think is the most important thing about their famous American. When they have decided this, they can begin their poems by starting them with the line:

The important thing about _____ is _____.

Remind the students to include some other facts from their web and to end their poems with the same line as the first line with the addition of the word *but*. As your students work on their poems, circulate and give them encouragement, reminding them to use the room and book resources to spell words and to circle words they couldn't find and don't think they spelled correctly. On the following day, you lead them to edit your poem and theirs.

Now, we have to edit our poems. We can use our editor's checklist.

Editor's Checklist

1. Do all the sentences make sense and stay on the topic?
2. Do all the sentences have appropriate ending punctuation?
3. Do all the sentences begin with capitals?
4. Are misspelled words circled?
5. Do all names start with capitals?

The students read your sentences one at a time and give you several thumbs up for each. They don't find any sentences that don't make sense or stay on the topic. They convince you to change the period at the end of the next to the last sentence to an exclamation mark. They note that all your sentences begin with caps but decide that Hoover and Atlantic Ocean are names and need capital letters.

> ### Amelia Earhart
>
> The important thing about Amelia Earhart is that she was a courageous woman.
>
> When she was growing up, everyone called her a tomboy.
>
> She was a nurse's aide in a military hospital during the first world war.
>
> She saw her first airplane at the Des Moines airshow when she was 10 years old.
>
> She became a pilot and bought an airplane.
>
> She named the airplane *The Canary.*
>
> She was the first woman to fly solo across the ᴬ⌃atlantic ᴼ⌃ocean.
>
> President ᴴ⌃hoover gave her a gold medal.
>
> She disappeared as she was trying to fly around the world
>
> She was never found!
>
> But the important thing about Amelia Earhart is that she was a courageous woman.

After the partners edit, you do a final edit, including fixing misspelled words they didn't notice or couldn't correct. The students copy their poems, download a picture from the Internet, and proudly display their poems on the Famous Americans Board just in time for open house.

What's New?

Another poetry format that will allow your students to share what they have learned about a topic uses a format we call *What's New?* It follows this pattern:

> What's New About _____?
>
> I already knew that _____
>
> But it's news to me that _____
>
> It is also interesting that _____
>
> But the coolest fact is that _____

Your class has been doing a unit on mammals and you decide the *What's New?* format will let them share what they already knew and what they learned. You choose a mammal and complete a simple chart planner.

Boys and girls, we have been studying mammals, and although I knew a lot about them, I have learned a lot of interesting facts I didn't know. We're going to make a classbook on mammals, and each person is going to choose one mammal to write a poem about. The poetry format we are going to use is called What's New? To help plan our poems, I have made a simple chart for you to fill in. Today, I am going to fill in this chart for the mammal I chose and then you can choose a mammal and fill in your chart. Tomorrow we will write our What's New? poems. The mammal I have chosen to write about is bats, so I will write *Bats* in the topic column.

Topic	Knew	News	Interesting	Coolest
Bats				

In the next column, I am going to write a few facts I already knew about bats before we started our unit on mammals. Before we started our unit, I knew that bats could fly, most lived in caves, and you could get rabies if they bit you.

Topic	Knew	News	Interesting	Coolest
Bats	Live in caves Fly Rabies			

Believe it or not, I never realized that bats were mammals. I guess because they could fly I thought they must be related to birds. But they are mammals. That was news to me.

Topic	Knew	News	Interesting	Coolest
Bats	Live in caves Fly Rabies	Mammals		

I'm going to skip to the last column, which is where you put the coolest fact you learned. For me, it was fascinating to learn that bats have echolocation, just like whales and dolphins and that is how they move around and locate their prey.

Topic	Knew	News	Interesting	Coolest
Bats	Live in caves Fly Rabies	Mammals		Echolocation like whales and dolphins Locate prey

Now, I just need to think of a few more interesting facts I want to include. There are many but I think it is very interesting that there are over 1,000 kinds of bats that live all over the world and that bats have been around for at least 50 million years.

Topic	Knew	News	Interesting	Coolest
Bats	Live in caves Fly Rabies	Mammals	1000 kinds all over the world 50,000,000 years	Echolocation like whales and dolphins Locate prey

Now, you need to choose the mammal you want to write about. You can choose any mammal except bats. Take a minute to talk with your partner about which mammal you will choose and why.

After a minute, ask a few students to tell you what mammal they have chosen. Then distribute the chart planner so they can begin planning what to write. Encourage them to use all the mammal books and magazines you have accumulated and to use these resources to help with spelling as well as ideas. Some of your students will likely have difficulty deciding what to include. Simply assure them that they can't tell everything they knew and learned but that they should just include the facts they think are surprising, interesting, and cool.

On the following day, show your students the What's New? poetry format.

What's New About _____?

I already knew that _____

But it's news to me that _____

It is also interesting that _____

But the coolest fact is that _____

Using the information on your chart planner and the What's New? format, you construct this poem as your students watch.

What's New About Bats?

I already knew that bats could fly lived in caves and could spread rabies.

But it's news to me that bats are mammals—not some kind of bird.

It is also interesting that there are over 1,000 kinds of bats who live all over the world and have been on earth for 50,000,000 years.

But the coolest fact is that bats have echolocation like dolphins and whales. Echolocation is how they hunt for their prey in the dark.

Having completed their planning chart and watched you write your poem and with the What's New? format displayed, your students will eagerly complete their What's New poems. On the following day, they help you edit your piece and work in partners with the editor's checklist to edit their pieces.

Your students decide that *Earth* should have a capital letter and (with a little help from you) they notice that the first sentence has things in a series and needs commas.

What's New About Bats?

I already knew that bats could fly, lived in caves, and could spread rabies.

But it's news to me that bats are mammals—not some kind of bird.

It is also interesting that there are over 1,000 kinds of bats who live all over the world and have been on **E**arth for 50,000,000 years.

But the coolest fact is that bats have echolocation like dolphins and whales. Echolocation is how they hunt for their prey in the dark.

Commas in a series has just been added to the editor's checklist and many students are not sure if their piece needs them or not. The editing partners try to work this out as you go around and coach them with this complex convention as they work.

Postcards

Did you know that the first postcards in the United States were printed by the U.S. Postal Service in 1873? For one cent, you could buy the card and that price included the cost for mailing. In fact, for many years postcards were known as penny postcards. (If you are a history/trivia buff, google the history of postcards and you will be amazed at the important communicative and artistic part postcards have played in our American journey.) *Postcards* is a short writing activity that allows you to focus on important conventions, including punctuating dates and addresses as you give your students an authentic writing purpose for sharing information. If you are studying your state or other states—including the various regions and important sites—you might want students to pretend they have taken a trip to one of these sites and they share what they learned through a postcard. Likewise, they could write postcards from Japan, Canada, Italy, or any other country or culture you might be studying.

Because postcards were the major way of communicating across this country before the days of telephones and email, settlers and immigrants used postcards to communicate with relatives they were never apt to see again. Imagine, for example, that you and your students have been reading some historical fiction set in the West in the post-Civil War era, including some of the *Little House on the Prairie* series by Laura Ingalls Wilder. Your students could assume the role of a child settling in the West who writes postcards to cousins back home describing how his or her life as a settler is different. Your students can experience vicariously the life of immigrant children if they are reading *Immigrant Kids* or other books about the immigrant experience by Russell Freedman or *If Your Name Was Changed at Ellis Island* or other books by Ellen Levine. Taking on the role of an immigrant child and writing postcards to distant relatives can help your students experience a different time and culture. Once you start to think about it, the possibilities for helping students communicate, sharpen their writing skills, and learn some important mechanics through postcards are pervasive in your social studies and literature curriculums.

Regardless of what venue you choose for incorporating postcards into your writing curriculum, you will want to model for your students the appropriate format for a postcard. After your students watch you write a postcard, they can write one, using your model for the format. The first draft should be written on a mock postcard. Once it is edited, the information can be written on a real postcard or one you create. (There are many sites on the Internet that enable you and your students to create snazzy-looking postcards.)

Before editing the postcards, you may want to add some comma rules to your editor's checklist if your students are at the place where they can begin to incorporate these into their automatic writing skills. An example on the checklist will make this convention much more understandable to most of your students.

Editor's Checklist

6. Are commas used to separate dates and places?

October 17, 1893   Richmond, Virginia

```
 _____
        date

Dear _____,                    stamp



                              To:


                              _____
                              _____
                              _____


        Yours truly,

        _____
```

Notes and Letters

Has anyone done something you and your students are all grateful for? Did the local fire department come and show off their equipment and talk to your students about fire safety? Perhaps one of your parents who works at a nursery came and shared some plant-growing tips as part of your science unit on plants. Is there a teacher or staff member at your school who coaches a sport or plays in a band or collects something and could share his or her interests and expertise with your students? Has the high school band played a concert for your class and shared some musical instrument information with your students? Has another class in your school put on a play for your students or shared some of their science projects?

Have you taken any fieldtrips recently? Fieldtrips don't have to be long, expensive affairs. Perhaps you could walk to a local grocery store and have the produce manager talk with your students about the nutritional value of all the tasty fruits and vegetables. Is there a business nearby that would welcome a visit from your class and explain how the business works and what the different employees do?

Has anyone donated anything to your class or school? Books? Baby chicks to hatch? Used computers and printers? Playground equipment? Do you have volunteers who regularly come to your room and help with science or art projects, publishing books or cooking experiences?

Visitors, fieldtrips, donations, volunteers, and special events are all opportunities for you to teach your students how to write thank-you notes. Thank-you notes are by nature short and to the point. Asking students to think of specific ways they are thankful will inspire students to think about what they learned or how they benefited from the experience. Finally, you can use thank-you notes to teach some simple letter formatting and some common comma uses.

Boys and girls, remember last week when the high school pep band came and played some music for us and told us about their instruments and how they learned to play them? I took some photos of the band members and I got Mr. Wood to write on these photos the name of each band member. I thought it would be fun to surprise Mr. Wood and all the band members with some thank-you notes telling them how much we enjoyed the music and how much we learned about the different instruments. Let's look at the photos and see what we can remember about the instruments these students were playing. Yes, these four students were all playing trumpets. How did the trumpets sound? What did the students tell you about how you play the trumpets?

The planning lesson continues as you record the names of instruments and a few comments about each in the columns of this chart.

Instrument	Characteristics
trumpet	Brass, blow air through tight lips, move 3 valves up and down to change pitch high and low sounds
trombone	Brass, blow air through tight lips, move slide up and down to change pitch mellow sounds
tuba	Brass
clarinet	Wind
saxaphone	Wind
snare drum	Percussion
bass drum	Percussion
cymbals	Percussion

I am going to write my note to Mr. Wood, the band director. After I write my note, you will each choose a band member's name and write a note to that person.

October 16, 2110

Dear Mr. Wood,

I can't tell you how much our class enjoyed having the hilltop pep band come to our school. The music was great. All my students were fasinated by the different instruments and talked all the next day about which instrument they want to play in your band when they get to high school. Thank you so much for halling all the band members and instruments here. We will all be cheering on the team on Friday night.

Your grateful friend,

Mrs. Cunningham

After you write your note, help your students notice the formatting of the greeting and the closing, including the commas. Students then write their first-draft notes on notebook paper to the band member they picked.

On the following day, the children use the Editor's Checklist to help you edit your piece. You fix the spelling of *fascinating* and *hauling*, begin *Hilltop* with a capital *H*, and change the period after *great* to an exclamation point.

October 16, 2110

Dear Mr. Wood,

I can't tell you how much our class enjoyed having the **H**hilltop pep band come to our school. The music was great! All my students were **fascinated** fasinated by the different instruments and talked all the next day about which instrument they want to play in your band when they get to high school. **hauling** Thank you so much for halling all the band members and instruments here. We will all be cheering on the team on Friday night.

Your grateful friend,

Mrs. Cunningham

The students then edit with their partners and you remind them that in addition to the items on the checklist, they should use your model to make sure the greeting and closing are in the right places and have commas. After a quick edit by the editor-in-chief, they copy their edited thank-you notes on notecards. After illustrating the notecards with a picture of the band instrument, the children put them in envelopes and write the band member's name to whom they have written the note. All the thank-you notes get put in one big envelope and are sent off to Mr. Wood and the Hilltop pep band.

October 13, 2010

Dear Carl,

Thank you for coming to our school and showing us how you play

the clarinet. It was very interesting to see how you play the high

different
notes and low notes by covering diffrent holes and changing how
vibration
much vibrasun there is. I will be looking for you when I go to the
F   B
game friday night. Go bulldogs!

Your friend,

Jacob Weigel

In addition to postcards and notes, depending on the age and writing sophistication of your students, you may want them to write letters. Letters give your students another opportunity to use the comma conventions that apply to dates and addresses. Friendly letters can tie into your literature curriculum as students write to favorite authors. Your social studies curriculum can also be enhanced as your students write letters as if they are living in an earlier time or a different place. Business letters can be written to request information about topics being studied and to express opinions about local issues such as pollution, recycling, and funding. As with all the short writing pieces described in this chapter, you should model planning, writing, and editing your piece and then lead the students through the planning, writing, and editing of their pieces. Be sure your students edit for whatever items you have on the editor's checklist and for the correct form.

Interviews

One source of information students enjoy collecting is often overlooked. There are many opportunities across the curriculum for your students to interview family, friends, and people in the community. History comes alive to your students if you send them out to interview the two oldest people they know about "life in the old days" or how the community has changed since they were growing up.

During a unit on the environment and recycling, you could send students to interview people about how they recycle things at work. If you do this interview, don't overlook the obvious. Dispatch some of your students around the school to interview the office staff, custodians, and cafeteria workers. What does your local library do about recycling? What about local businesses, including convenience stores and restaurants?

Math is an area that students often think of as part of the school world and not the real world. The reality is that people use math in their jobs and to accomplish everyday tasks. Your students will enjoy interviewing family members, neighbors and local business owners, and perhaps develop more interest in math as they realize the role it plays in everyone's adult life. Share the results of the interview with your cousin.

I got some surprising answers to my questions about how people use math every day to get things done. When I interviewed my cousin who works at the lumberyard, he talked about how important it is to measure and to estimate how much paint and other materials people will need. "You would be amazed how many people come in to buy things without measuring the space they are working with first. I have to send them home to get their measurements and then we do the math to make sure they are buying enough—but not too much."

Another reason for including some interviews across the school year is that they are the perfect opportunity for students to learn how to punctuate quotes in their writing. As you help them plan for their interviews, tell your students that they need to include at least one quote from each person they interview. Model this as you write up the results of your interview and add punctuating quotations to your editor's checklist if it is not already there. Be sure to include an example of a quote on your checklist.

Word Problems

Think-writes work naturally into your daily math instruction, but it is more difficult to come up with genuine writing assignments you might give your students in
math that need editing. Remember that the purpose of editing is to make the writing
easier to read. Although we do a lot of writing in math to help us clarify our thinking, this is writing for ourselves, not for others. One kind of writing activity you can
include regularly in your math curriculum is to have your students write math problems for other students to solve. Students, however, are often not enthusiastic about
this activity and the word problems they create are often too easy, too hard, or don't
contain enough information. You can solve this problem, though, if you give your
students a sheet with some numbers to add, subtract, multiply, or divide. Be sure
that the numbers you include are appropriate to the level of math your students are
working on. The numbers you give them to compute should include some that have
the same numbers but different operations are required. Imagine that you give your
students the accompanying sheet of math computations.

1. 23 − 9	2. 23 + 9	3. 23 × 9	4. 23 ÷ 9
5. 16 + 8	6. 16 − 8	7. 16 × 8	8. 16 ÷ 8
9. 37 ÷ 5	10. 37 + 5	11. 37 × 5	12. 37 − 5
13. 15 × 6	14. 15 − 6	15. 15 + 6	16. 15 ÷ 6
17. 52 ÷ 4	18. 52 × 4	19. 52 + 4	20. 52 − 4
21. 20 − 3	22. 20 ÷ 3	23. 20 × 3	24. 20 + 3
25. 62 + 7	26. 62 × 7	27. 62 − 7	28. 62 ÷ 7
29. 64 − 2	30. 64 + 2	31. 64 × 2	32. 64 ÷ 2

Tell your students that you are going to make up some math problems and
their job is to decide which one of the computations on the sheet to use. Write the
problem and use the names of your students in each problem.

Kevin is saving money to buy a new video game. He has $9.00 saved and the video game costs $23.00. How much more money does he need to save?

Erin bought two dozen cookies to share with all her friends. She gave one cookie to her dog. Eight friends came over to her house that afternoon. How many cookies can each person have? How many will be left for Erin to eat or feed her dog?

Boys and girls, who knows which item number on the math sheet we will use to figure out how much more money Kevin needs to save? Yes, we will use number 1. Subtract 9 from 23 and see how much more money Kevin needs to save.

Which one will we use to solve Erin's problem? This one is trickier. Can anyone tell me how many cookies are in two dozen? Yes—12 cookies in one dozen, 24 in two—but remember she gave her dog one cookie. Good thinking. Erin has 23 cookies to divide between 9 people (including herself). That is number 4 on the math sheet. See if you can solve that one. How many cookies will each person get and how many will Erin have left?

Now, I want each of you to write two math problems that can be solved with two different computations. When you have written them, work with your editing partner to edit for the items on the checklist—including that you have a question mark after your question. Then bring your problems to me. I will do a final edit. Later, I will type them and they will be your math work for tomorrow. Use each other's names if you like, but remember that we never say or write anything negative about anyone in our class.

Carl has a bag of candy he wants to share with his six friends. They count the candy and there are 62 pieces. How many pieces of candy will Carl and his friends get? How many will be left for his sister?

Liz invites 15 friends to her birthday party. Six friends get sick and can't come. How many friends came to her party?

David collects toy cars. He has 52 cars. How many wheels are on all the cars put together?

Paul is at his family reunion. There are 64 people there when his grandma and grandpa arrive. How many people are now at the reunion?

Looking Back
Writing and Editing across the Curriculum

When you have your students write across the curriculum, you create a win-win situation. Your students' writing skills improve because they are writing more and they learn more because writing is another avenue for working with new ideas. Because the short pieces students write are meant to be read by others, they need to be edited. As you model the planning, writing, and editing of these pieces, students learn how to write a variety of forms and the editing conventions these forms require. Some of the formats that work well across the curriculum include:

- Cinquain poetry
- Important Poems
- What's New? poems
- Postcards
- Thank-you notes
- Letters
- Interviews
- Math word problems

Chapter 7

Revision Matters!

What is revision and how does it differ from editing? As explained in Chapter 5, editing is proofreading and correcting a paper for errors in spelling, mechanics, and usage. In contrast, revising is improving a paper by making changes in meaning, organization, or style.

Someone else can edit for you, but only authors can revise. Once an editor begins revising an author's paper, that person has ceased being its editor and has become its coauthor.

Revision is more important, less exact, and more difficult to do and learn than editing. Imagine that scientists invent a "correct writing" chip that all children have implanted in their brains when they start first grade. For the rest of their lives, they make no errors in spelling, capitalization, punctuation, or usage. Would that make them good writers? Would readers understand everything they wrote? Would readers be interested in everything they wrote? Would readers be persuaded by everything they wrote? The purpose of revision is not to teach writers how to make their papers more correct, but rather to make their writing more comprehensible, more appealing, more convincing, and so on. As you read a paper that needs revising, you might find yourself thinking such thoughts as:

"I don't get what the point is."

"I'm having trouble following this."

"I wish she would give an example of this."

"This information is not very well organized."

"The ending is a real letdown."

The need for revision is often just as obvious when listening to a paper as when reading it, because revision is all about the meaning and how clear and cleverly that meaning is conveyed in language.

Do you like to revise your writing? Do you like helping your students revise their writing? A few people might earnestly answer "Yes!" to these questions, but for many of us (the authors of this book included!), revising is the hardest part of writing. Yet, all published writers revise and all high-quality writing has been revised. Students must learn to regard revising not as a chore but as an essential part of writing that can make their good writing even better! Many teachers must also undergo an "attitude adjustment" about revising and approach it enthusiastically. Remember, attitudes matter and are highly contagious. In this chapter, we will try to convince you that revising is necessary, is do-able, and produces more satisfying results. You can then approach your students with an attitude toward revision that will help many of them "catch" your enthusiasm.

Revision Starts When the Writer Rereads the Paper to Make It Even Better

Writers do many things as they revise but the most essential thing and the starting point for any revision is captured by the word *revise* itself. The word is made up of the prefix *re*, meaning "again," and the Latin root *vis*, meaning "to see or look." When writers revise, they look again at their writing, and ask the essential question: "How can I make this piece of writing *even* better?"

The word *even* in this question is important because it implies that the writing may already be good but can be even better! Using the phrase *even better* is part of the attitude adjustment you and your students may need to make about revising, since many children think that having to revise means they didn't do a good job to begin with. All successful writers revise and all published writing has been revised, however good the first draft was. Writers always begin revising by rereading their writing, and thinking about how to make it *even* better.

Sometimes writers revise on their own—by themselves. We all do some revising whenever we think of a better word, or realize our beginning will not grab the attention of the reader, and then stop to rework the first few sentences or paragraphs. Most writers reread their writing when it is finished, or sometime later, and make some changes to make the piece better. Before publishing a piece, however, most writers need someone else to read the piece while asking the "How could it be even better?" question. Conferring with another person who has read what you have written often helps you see how you can improve your piece of writing in ways you didn't think of as you reread it. If your reader ignores your spelling and conventions errors and focuses instead on your paper's meaning, organization, and style, the feedback you get from that reader can be invaluable in helping you find some things to revise to improve your paper. (Of course, later, that same reader or a different one can help you edit your revised first draft.)

When to Teach Revision

Even with older children, it is easy to start revision too early in the year. As we explained in Chapter 5, we don't ask students to edit until most of them have developed some self-confidence, intrinsic motivation, and independence in first-draft writing. Similarly, we don't ask students to revise until most of them have developed some ability in editing. Once students are confident in their writing and have some skill with editing their own papers individually or in partners, they are more willing and able to learn also to revise them.

Why We Teach Editing Before We Teach Revision

Many children think revising and editing are the same thing. Unless they are given the opportunity to learn to edit their own papers before they are expected also to revise them, many of them will just edit when you want them to revise. Once your students understand what editing is, have learned how to do it with a basic editor's checklist, and have practiced taking several papers through a writing process with an editing step but not a revision step, then they will understand and can be persuaded when you introduce revising as different from editing. Most of your students will not feel the need to edit during revision as much when they know what editing is and that they will have the chance to do it *after* they revise.

Who can tell me what editing means? Yes, when we edit, we fix our writing. We change our sentences if they don't make sense or sound right. We make sure we have punctuation and capitals in the right places. We fix the spelling. Editing is fixing your writing so it is easier for readers to read.

Today, we are going to begin learning to revise. When we revise our writing, we make it even better. We change some words to more descriptive words. There is nothing wrong with these words. They are spelled correctly and they make sense but more descriptive words will make our writing even better. Sometimes when we revise, we add more detail that lets our readers really experience whatever we are writing about. Sometimes, we rearrange some of our sentences or paragraphs to make the meaning clearer and easier to understand.

Revising is not fixing mistakes. Fixing mistakes is editing. Revising is adding, changing, and rearranging that will make our writing even better and easier to understand. When we revise, we don't worry about editing. After we revise, we will do the editing steps we have learned to do. Then, when we publish our writing, everyone will marvel at what wonderful writers we are!

Modeling revising and editing, in that order, in several mini-lessons will help your students learn to distinguish between the two and when it is appropriate to do each. It is also important to remind them repeatedly that if they edit a paper before they revise it, they will just have to edit it *again*, since they will probably have new errors in the changes they make during revision. Since no one wants to have to edit twice, when we revise, writers always revise *before* they edit.

Teaching Your Students the Four General Revising Strategies

Every teacher of writing has met resistance from students when asking them to revise their papers. We have already mentioned the possibility that both teachers and students may need an "attitude adjustment" toward revision. It is even more important for you to make sure your students know what revising is and how to do it. Vague admonitions to "make it better, clearer, and more interesting" have always been a source of frustration to all writers—children and adults alike.

In Chapter 5, you learned how to help your students edit with a partner. Students also need to learn how to revise with a partner. Partner editing is easier than partner revising, however, because editing partners have an editing checklist and know exactly what to look for. Because revision improves meaning, organization, or style, rather than correcting errors in spelling or conventions, it is much harder for your students to know what they are looking for when they read their own or their partner's paper. You can help them, however, by teaching them the four general revising strategies: adding, replacing, removing, and reordering. Learning these strategies helps them understand what revision is, how it is different from editing, and where to begin when trying to make the meaning, organization, or style of a selected piece of writing even better.

After their peer partners and you help your students decide what is needed to make the meaning, organization, or style of their first draft even better, they can revise that draft by adding, replacing, removing, or reordering. Sometimes they add, replace, or reorder some words or phrases, or remove one or more words or phrases. Sometimes they add, replace, or reorder some sentences or paragraphs, or remove one or more sentences or paragraphs. Occasionally, a writer will add, replace, or reorder some sections, or remove an entire section that is already there. (Lori Rog in her truly marvelous book titled *Marvelous Minilessons for Teaching Beginning Writing, K–3* uses kid-friendly language to describe these procedures. She refers to adding as "pushing in," replacing is "trading," reordering is "cutting and sorting," and removing is "chopping out." We think this kid-friendly language makes revising less scary and will use it as we describe some of our mini-lessons.)

Just as you did with editing, you will model and demonstrate the four revising strategies during mini-lessons and then support your students doing the strategies in their own papers with the help of a partner. And, just as with editing, revising strategies are taught gradually. When your students have been taught only one strategy, they are expected to use only that one strategy.

Once revising begins, it becomes the first things partners do—before they edit. Helping your students revise also becomes the first focus of your instruction during writing conferences. As you conference with students getting ready to publish, and as they work with their partners, you remind them of the revising strategies you have taught them so far and give them help implementing one or two of these with their piece.

You will choose revision strategies to teach to your class that you believe most of your students are ready to learn. During writing conferences, however, you can differentiate instruction. When your students conference with you about their first drafts, you can suggest and help individual writers who are ready to make their piece even better by using a strategy not yet taught to the whole class.

Teaching the Adding (Pushing In) Revising Strategy

Adding is the easiest revising strategy to learn and thus we teach it first. Children are often impressed with themselves when they write a long piece—and adding makes any first draft longer and more impressive! By starting with the adding revising strategy, you can capitalize on your students' affinity for length and start them off with a positive attitude toward revising.

If you have been writing on every other line during your mini-lessons and having your children write on every other line on all their first drafts, adding just a word, phrase or sentence will be easy to do right on the original piece. Adding longer sections will require cutting and taping—something children love to do, which also helps improve their attitude toward revising.

Revising by Adding Words or Phrases

Here is a mini-lesson in which children learn that adding words or phrases can make the meaning and style of their piece clearer and more vivid. To do this mini-lesson, find a piece you wrote recently and pull it back out. Tell your students that you want to revise this piece before you publish it and that one way to revise is to add a few words or phrases that make the meaning clearer or that make the writing "come alive."

> Boys and girls, do you remember last week when I wrote the newsletter article describing what we were learning from our virtual fieldtrips to Japan? I was getting ready to type this piece into the newsletter you will take home on Friday and I realized I had not put in very many details. So, I am going to make this piece of writing even better by pushing in some details that will help your parents visualize more clearly what we saw on our virtual fieldtrips.

Use a bright-color marker and show your students how you put a ∧ (called a caret) and then insert a word or phrase (or short sentence) in the empty line above at two or three different places to make what you have written clearer or more vivid. Once you have revised the piece, have your students read it with you and help you explain how the added words and phrases make it better or clearer.

Our Trip to Japan

Have you ever been to Japan? Have you ever wanted to go there? This

month, our class has been planning and taking virtual fieldtrips to

Japan. Here are just a few of the things we have learned.

Japan is a beautiful country. It is made up of four large islands plus
about the size of California ∧

hundreds of medium and small islands. We took a virtual climb up
a dormant volcano and
Mount Fuji, ∧ the tallest mountain in Japan. The view just kept getting

better the higher we went!

Did you know that there were real ninja? Ninja were warriors who
used martial arts and
∧ lived centuries ago.

We took a virtual fieldtrip to the annual festival at a Shinto shrine.
The priests carried the god of the shrine.
∧ There were decorated floats and thousands of worshippers.

Our virtual fieldtrips have taught us a lot about Japan. We would all

like to travel there someday for real!

Over the next several days, demonstrate adding words or phrases to revise with a few more of your pieces or with a piece volunteered by a student. Whenever you use a student's piece, be sure it is a relatively good piece of writing and that you have the child's enthusiastic permission to use it. Make a transparency of the student's writing and use the same procedure. Monitor the writer's reaction as you revise this paper and finish quickly if you note any discomfort.

When you have done enough mini-lessons to be sure that most of your students understand revising by adding words or phrases, partner them up so that children of relatively equal writing ability are working together. Ask each partner to choose a piece of his or her writing and to suggest words or phrases to each other that will make their two pieces of writing clearer or more vivid. Give them brightly colored pens and christen these as "revising pens." Collect the pens when the partners are finished revising their two papers and reserve them only for revising. The children will enjoy using these bright special pens and this too will have a positive effect on their attitude toward revising.

As your students revise, go around and help the partners who seem to be having trouble adding words and phrases you have taught them in your mini-lessons. As you move around the room, monitoring and helping the partners, be on the lookout for particularly good additions. When the writing time is over, gather your students together and have them share some of the best revisions you noticed.

I moved here with my family in 2005. **because of hurricane Katrina.** We used to live with my ∧

grandfather in New Orleans. The hurricane flooded his house and we had to go to the superdome. **We had to leave our cat.** ∧ It was dark and wet inside. **The bathrooms didn't work.** ∧ We got

hungry and thirsty. We were scared. It was a long time until we got

to leave the Superdome. We stayed in Hooston **Texas** ∧ until we moved up

here.

Revising by Adding Dialogue

Another way of making writing clearer and more vivid by adding is to add dialogue. Again, take one of your pieces and use it as the first example. (You might want to plan ahead and write a piece with no dialogue but that would be improved by inserting a few statements of exact words at different places, so that you have a good example to use later for this revision mini-lesson.)

Who remembers what I did to the Japan piece in the newsletter last week to make it even better? Yes, I added a few words and phrases to make the piece more vivid and to help your parents visualize what we saw. Another way to make your writing come alive is to add some dialogue—the words people or characters actually say. Today I am going to revise my piece on "Hiking" by pushing in some dialogue.

Use the same procedure that you used with adding words and phrases, except now you will provide a brief explanation of how quotations are punctuated. However, make sure that your emphasis is on how adding dialogue can improve the meaning and make it more interesting, not on how quotations are punctuated. How to punctuate quotations correctly is taught and practiced during the editing step of the writing process, not during the revision step.

My Hiking Adventure

When I was your age, I went to a state park with my family. We went
My mother told my brothers and me, "Hiking is fun and good for you."
hiking on a trail. My legs were shorter than everyone else's and I fell

I screamed, "Help me!"
behind. I slipped on the trail and slid down an embankment into a

thicket. I was caught on briars and couldn't get loose. My father came
"Daddy, daddy," I called as loud as I could.
looking for me in a little while. He heard me yelling but couldn't figure

out where I was. Finally, he and my older brother found me. It took them
My mother said, "I guess hiking isn't always fun!"
a long time to get me loose from the briars.

Do a few more mini-lessons in which you use your writing or the writing volunteered by one of your students to demonstrate how adding dialogue makes the writing more dramatic. Partner up your students and have them help each other find a place where adding dialogue will make their writing even better. Spy on the partners, helping those who seem to need it, and select a few good examples of revisions to share with the whole class afterwards.

Revising by Adding a Missing Part

So far, we have learned to add by pushing in a few descriptive words and phrases and some dialogue. Sometimes, once we finish our first draft, we realize we have left out an important part. We don't have enough room to add this part in where it needs to go. Today I will show you how some scissors and tape can help us solve our problem and add an important part.

Begin this mini-lesson, like the other "adding" mini-lessons, with a previously written first draft. For your first mini-lesson of this kind, make sure your first draft obviously lacks important information somewhere in the middle. For example, if your first draft is a narrative telling about a vacation you took to an amusement park close to where you live, it could relate how you traveled to the amusement park and how you returned home, yet tell almost nothing about what you actually saw and did at the amusement park. When you ask your students to read your first draft and make suggestions about how you could make it better, you want it to be highly likely that several of them will suggest that you need to tell them more than you have and that the missing part needs to be added somewhere in the middle, rather than at the beginning or the end of your first draft.

Once everyone has agreed that there is important information missing, have the students help you decide exactly where to add the new part. Then, as they watch you, use a pair of scissors to cut your first draft into a beginning and ending right at the place where the addition will go. Next, put a clean piece of acetate on the overhead and compose the addition while they watch you. Be sure to position the beginning of your first draft so they can see that your addition continues nicely from it. As soon as you have written the first sentence or two of your addition, you can lay the beginning of the first draft aside. Finish your addition, letting them help you decide when you have told them enough that is new. After completing the addition, use cellophane tape to tape the beginning of your first draft to the top of your addition and the end of your first draft to the bottom of your addition. Your revised first draft will now probably be as long as two pieces of acetate taped together, so you will need to gradually move the entire taped sheet up as they read your revised first draft. After they have read it, ask them if they think it is more complete and better now than it was before you revised. Hopefully, most of them will agree that it is.

After you have done one of these cut-and-tape mini-lessons, you will find that several of your students will want to do what you have done. Ask your students to look at their first drafts and try to find one with a chunk of missing information at the beginning, in the middle, or at the end. If your students need to add a part before their first draft begins or after it ends, they won't need to cut their first draft, but they will need to tape their addition to it. On several subsequent days, do mini-lessons with pieces that your students volunteer or with other pieces you write where you cut and tape or just tape to add a missing part. You will soon find that your students love to cut and tape and will be eager to find a place in a piece they are going to publish that needs more information so they can get to work on it with scissors and tape.

At first, the beginnings, middles, or ends they add may not be wonderful, but your students can still meet the two goals of instruction in revising by adding a missing part. The first goal is that they start developing the sense that every piece of writing needs a distinct beginning, middle, and end. Of course, all children have been told that they need these three parts when they write, but they will only begin to understand what this really means and to take it seriously if they learn how to notice when one of these parts is missing from their own first draft, and then work to add it.

The second goal achieved by cutting and taping a missing part to their first draft is that they and you begin to talk about the importance of a good beginning and end. At first, you should keep this conversation at a very basic and common-sense level. Later, when your students learn to revise by replacing their beginning or ending, will be a better time to teach your students a more sophisticated sense of how to begin and end a draft. In other words, it is enough at first to make sure students' papers have a distinct beginning, middle, and end, rather than being concerned with how good the beginnings and endings are!

My favorite book is Tom Sawyer by Mark Twain.

The main character was an orphan named Tom Sawyer. He and his little brother lived with their Aunt Polly. They lived in a little town on the frontier in the 18 hundreds. It was the time of slavery. It was on the Mississippi River in the state of Missouri. The children went to a one-room school. Except for Huck. He didn't go to school.

Tom tricked the other boys so they washed the fense Aunt Polly was making him wash. They even paid him to let them wash it! He tricked his teacher by buying tickets from boys that learned there bible verses so he could win. Becky's father found out and he got in big trouble. He tricked the teacher into whipping him instead of Becky so Becky would love him. I was scared when Tom and Huck hid in the grave yard and saw the murder. The most exciting part is when Tom and Becky get lost in the cave and Injun Joe is in there, too!

At this point, you may want to begin a *Revising Chart* to post in your room to remind children of the revising strategies writers use. Here is an example of what it might look like at this stage.

Revising—Making your Writing EVEN Better

Look again at your writing. Pick a friend to look with you.

Use special revising pens or cut and tape.

Add (Push in):

    Words that make the writing more vivid or clearer

    Dialogue that makes the writing come alive

    Missing information

Adding details, dialogue, or a missing part are all examples of the general revision strategy of adding. It is usually the easiest way for writers to revise and so we teach it first. Children are motivated to find places to add by the lure of special colored pens and scissors and tape. As they practice revising by adding, they are encouraged when they find that their revised drafts are longer and more mature looking. Once your students can revise by adding, you may begin teaching them the most important general revision strategy—replacing.

Teaching the Replacing (Trading) Revising Strategy

Replacing (trading) is another revising strategy all proficient writers use. Whereas the adding strategy makes writing better by making it more elaborate and complete, the replacing strategy makes writing better by improving the quality of what is already there. As with adding, you can replace words or phrases, sentences, or a whole chunk of text. When replacing a small amount of text, use the special revising pens to cross out the text that needs improvement and write the new text clearly above it. When replacing large chunks in order to improve them, use the cut and tape procedure.

Revising by Replacing Words or Phrases

Writers are always seeking "just the right word"—the word that will communicate exactly what they mean. Looking again at their writing and asking themselves the "How can I make it *even* better?" question often leads writers to replace common or overused words with other more descriptive, more vivid words. Here is a mini-lesson designed to teach children how to revise by replacing words.

Write something for your students and use as many boring, tired, and common words as you can. Don't tell your students your intent ahead of time. Just write it as you normally write during a mini-lesson.

This spring we were happy to move into a new house. But, we were sad to leave the good neighbors we had at our old house. The Ahmeds were nice to us after our kitchen caught on fire five years ago. They cooked food for us and let us use their kitchen until we redid ours. The Garcias were good neighbors, too. Their children fed and walked our dog when we went out of town.

When you finish, have the class read it with you and ask them if they can think of any ways you can make your writing even better. Since you have already taught several mini-lessons on revising by adding, they may suggest some words or phrases for you to add. It is all right to quickly add a few of the words suggested, but if no one also suggests replacing some of your "overused" words, you will need to suggest it yourself in order to move your mini-lesson from the adding to the replacing strategy:

> I notice that I have some common words here that don't create very vivid pictures. "*Nice*, for example, doesn't really describe how our neighbors were after our kitchen was damaged by fire. I think I will cross out *nice* and replace it with *generous*.

Continue replacing some of your boring, overused, or inexact words, eliciting suggestions from your students about which words need replacing and what you could replace them with. Be sure to convey your enthusiasm for "just the right word" when they have helped you find one. Your students need to change from seeing uncommon words as occasions for making a spelling error to opportunities for expressing themselves in a clear and enjoyable way.

---

                thrilled
     This spring we were ~~happy~~ to move into a new house. But, we were
down in the dumps   caring
 ~~sad~~ to leave the ~~good~~ neighbors we had at our old house. The Ahmeds
       generous
were ~~nice~~ to us after our kitchen caught on fire five years ago. They
prepared
~~cooked~~ food for us and let us use their kitchen until we redid ours. The
          fantastic
Garcias were ~~good~~ neighbors, too. Their children fed and walked our

dog when we went out of town.

You may also want to choose a paragraph from one of your students' favorite authors who uses lots of descriptive words and rewrite it by changing the descriptive words to boring, overused, or inexact words. Here is a paragraph rewritten in this way from *Little Women* by Lousia May Alcott:

Mr. Cunningham's Boring Version

The fire burned brightly within. It was a nice old room, though the carpet was old and the furniture very simple. A good picture or two hung on the walls, books filled the empty places, flowers grew in the windows, and a nice feeling of safety filled it.

After rewriting this paragraph, explain to your students that your boring version may even be like the way the author first wrote the paragraph. Perhaps the author looked back at it and decided she had used a lot of boring words. Let your students find the boring words and think of replacements. Write these replacements above any words they tell you and then compare the revised paragraph with the one from the actual book by reading that paragraph to them. (Make sure your students understand that we don't actually know that the author had written a less vivid draft and then revised it by replacing words.)

Louisa May Alcott's Original

"The fire crackled cheerfully within. It was a comfortable old room, though the carpet was faded and the furniture very plain. A good picture or two hung on the walls, books filled the recesses, chrysanthemums and Christmas roses bloomed in the windows, and a pleasant atmosphere of home-peace pervaded it."

Children often think that a wonderful writer just happens to be able to write well. They need to be reminded that all writers revise and the best writers do the most revision. Finish each lesson by reading the actual paragraph from the book and comparing the boring version, your students' revisions, and the author's actual final words.

Just as with revising by adding, you probably will need to do several mini-lessons on replacing words or phrases before asking your students to use this strategy in one of their papers. Again, when they try to apply the strategy to their own writing, have them work in partners as you move around, helping individuals having trouble, and look for good examples of revision to share with everyone afterwards.

Revising by Replacing "Telling" with "Showing"

"Show, don't tell" is a basic guideline for good writing. Unfortunately, many children (and adults!) are not sure what this guideline means. To teach your students what it means, you will have to practice what you preach and *show* them how to "Show, don't tell" instead of taking the far easier road of *telling* them to "Show, don't tell!"

To teach our young writers to replace telling words with words and sentences that "show," we use many of the procedures already described in this chapter. We write pieces in which we purposely tell rather than show and then revise these pieces in mini-lessons with our students' help. We use paragraphs from our students' favorite authors as examples and rewrite these for use in mini-lessons by replacing the showing words with telling words and sentences. After identifying the places where the children wish the writer had shown them rather than told them, we read the original and compare the "telling" version with the "showing" version. After several mini-lessons, we partner students up and ask them to help each other find examples in their writing where they could make the writing come alive by replacing some of their telling words with showing words and sentences.

Original

My brother Eddie was one of the stars of the game. He helped us win. It looked like we was going to lose, but we won at the last minute! We stayed after the game to watch the ceremony. It was neat!

Revised Version after Replacing Telling by Showing

My brother Eddie was one of the stars of the game. He helped us win. There was 20 secunds to go. We was down by 1 point. We was too far away to kick a fieldgoal. Eddies the left end. He ran back and got the ball from the quarterback and ran around the right end. The defence was all chasing him. They tackled him on the 10. Then we kicked a fieldgoal and won the game! We stayed after the game to watch the ceremony. It was neat!

Revising by Replacing the Beginning

For most children, the first revision they do that replaces a chunk of text is when they make the beginning of a piece noticeably better. Why does the beginning of a first draft so often need replacing? Because writers rarely know what kind of beginning would be best until they have written the middle and the end. Yes, planning a first draft before writing it often makes it better, but good writing also involves discovery. No matter how well writers plan a first draft, they never know exactly what they will say and how they will solve the problems that inevitably arise until they actually do the writing. Sometimes writers don't discover their voices for a particular topic or story until halfway through the piece!

Some students lack a beginning to their first draft and have to revise by adding one; others have a distinct beginning that is either a poor beginning or too much of a beginning! A poor beginning often gives away the middle and ending so that there is really no need to read the rest or it doesn't relate very well to the middle and ending. A beginning is "too much" when it goes on and on, previewing what is coming or building background beyond what is necessary for the readers.

The trick in helping your students learn how to replace their beginnings with better ones is to teach them what an excellent beginning is. It does little good to tell most students that they should have a better beginning; they need to know what a better beginning for this piece might be.

An excellent beginning tells readers what they need to know to understand the middle and end. The single-most important thing that a good beginning does is to build background knowledge for the readers so they will understand the middle and end. If the piece of writing is any kind of a narrative, the beginning must tell when and where the narrative begins (the setting). The beginning must also describe or explain what the readers are going to need to know about the time and place in order to understand the narrative.

When the writing is about a topic, the topic must be identified in the beginning so readers will know what it is. Then, background knowledge about the topic must be built so readers are ready to understand what the writer will say about the topic in the middle and end of the piece.

An excellent beginning makes readers want to keep reading. There are four main ways that good writers grab readers' attention and keep them reading. You can grab your reader's attention by beginning with a surprising fact:

There are more than 1,000 different kinds of bats in the world.

Mrs. Cunningham's fourth-graders filled seven huge bags with trash during the lake clean-up this weekend.

Imagine how the people who crossed the country in a wagon train that took six months would react to our impatience with a six-hour flight.

Another way to grab the readers' interest is to start with a quote:

"Help, I'm stuck in here and I can't get out," yelled my cousin, Carl.

"If we don't get rescued soon, we will starve to death," sighed the stranded sailor.

"You are the wettest puppy I ever saw," I marvelled. "Where did you come from?"

Starting with a question is also a way to engage readers:

Did you ever wonder who invented the piano?

What would you do if you found a lost puppy and your mom said you couldn't keep it?

Have you ever smelled a skunk?

Students also have to learn that if they start with a question, they must resist the temptation to answer or even begin to answer the question in the following sentence. Rather, now that they have the readers' attention, they need to build some background so that the rest of the piece will be clear and make sense to the readers.

Another way that good writers make readers want to keep reading is to start in the middle of things.

As Marsha and Gomez sat down to dinner, a large riderless motorcycle crashed through the front wall of their house, knocking them and their dinners to the floor.

That beginning will make most readers want to keep reading. Like starting with a question, after a writer begins a piece in the middle of things, then the writer must step back and build the background knowledge necessary for readers to understand what will follow.

The second sentence—one that keeps the readers' attention but begins to tell the background of the story—might be

They didn't have time to remember the anonymous threat they had received in the mail two days before.

Your students can try to start the first draft of a narrative they are writing in the middle of things, but they will usually have a better beginning of this kind when they write it during revision. As we have said, the best beginnings are based on the writer knowing what will be said in the middle and end of the piece and that can only fully occur during a separate revision step that follows the writing of a first draft.

Revising by Replacing the Ending

Any writer can tell you that good endings are hard to write! Children often solve the problem by stopping when they can't think of anything else to say and writing "The End." Consequently, you should have already helped your students to revise by adding an ending that was missing from the first draft. We find that it is easier to get most students to end a piece than it is to get them to end it well. That is why teaching your students to revise by replacing their ending will help almost all of them to write even better and more interesting endings than they do now. Again, of course, we must not rely on telling children that they need a better ending; rather, we must strive to teach them what makes an excellent ending.

An excellent ending answers the readers' questions or shows why they can't be answered. One of the best kinds of mini-lessons to help your students replace their ending with a better one is to have them read a piece with the ending covered up and then decide as a group on the two or three most important questions they want the ending to answer. Once they have posed these questions for you to write down, then have them read the ending to decide whether their questions are answered. If they asked a good question that is not answered, ask them to decide whether the ending made it clear why that question couldn't be answered. The discussion should end with suggestions for how the ending could be changed so it does answer all their most important questions or show why one or more of them can't be answered.

After several mini-lessons of this kind, your students should be able to work in partners to read several of their first drafts and decide what questions readers of each would probably want the ending to answer. They then should each revise an ending that doesn't answer these questions by replacing it with one that does, or show why the questions can't be answered.

An excellent ending should feel right to readers. It may seem simple, but one of the most valuable experiences for helping your students write better endings is for them to engage in discussions about whether they like the ending to a particular piece of writing and why or why not. These discussions should begin only after several of the mini-lessons on making sure the ending answers the most important questions that remain in the reader's mind, but endings can answer these questions without the answers being satisfying. There are no rules for what makes an end "feel right" to readers, and readers will never completely agree with each other, but good writers have a sense of what readers will enjoy. Certainly, your children want their classmates to like what they write. Discussions of whether they liked an ending, why or why not, and what would have made it one they liked more, will help students develop this sense of what their audience wants and doesn't want.

An excellent ending can surprise the reader but not too much. The third insight that we want to give students about what makes for an excellent ending is that it often surprises the reader. The reason it is the last of the three to teach is that it is an insight that is definitely prone to abuse. Armed with this idea, many children will leap to replace their ending with one that surprises, but that raises more questions than it answers and does not satisfy. An ending can surprise the reader, and is probably better if it does, but the surprise cannot be so great that it leaves the reader saying, "What? Where did that come from? I don't get it." It's probably best to give examples of good surprise endings and bad surprise endings and talk with the children about what makes for a good one.

Revising—Making your Writing EVEN Better

Look again at your writing. Pick a friend to look with you.

Use special revising pens or cut and tape.

Add (Push in):

    Words that make the writing more vivid or clearer

    Dialogue that makes the writing come alive

    Missing information

Replace (Trade):

    Boring words

    Telling with showing

    Beginnings that don't grab the readers' attention

    Endings that don't answer the readers' questions

Teaching the Reordering (Cutting and Sorting) Revising Strategy

Revising by reordering is not a common revising strategy and should not be taught until students can revise by adding and revise by replacing. Moreover, children cannot learn to revise by reordering until they have a firm sense of sequence and logical order—a sense that many children do not develop until third grade. This revising strategy is probably best taught individually, when the need arises in a particular paper. If you teach third grade or higher, and if your students are able to revise by adding and by replacing, be on the lookout for opportunities to help individuals improve their papers by reordering sentences, paragraphs, or sections. Also be aware that a narrative that begins in the middle of things can usually be achieved through revising by reordering. An exciting event can be moved from the middle or end of the first draft, and then followed with background from or a flashback to what was originally in the beginning of the first draft.

Teaching the Removing (Chopping Out) Revising Strategy

Just as children like to add because it makes their piece longer, they don't like to remove anything because they worked hard to write it and it shortens their piece if they take it out. Students are usually more willing to replace something than just remove it. This is the reason why removing is the last of the four general revising strategies you should teach.

Often, however, when more mature writers finish writing something, we realize that something we included does not really add anything to our writing or distracts the reader from the points we are trying to make. None of us likes to delete the wonderful words we have written, but deleting or removing off-topic or distracting sentences or paragraphs is an essential revising strategy. When we do teach it, we begin like we teach the other general revision strategies, with mini-lessons and guided practice in partners.

When your students have developed as writers and as revisers to the point that it is time to teach them the strategy of revising by removing, setting a maximum length for a revised paper can be extremely useful. It works like this. First, use examples from newspapers and magazines to show the students that published writers often need to convey a lot of information in a short space. Also, help your students experience and understand that they do not enjoy reading something that goes on and on without making its points in an efficient fashion. Second, when you think you have helped your students become sensitive to the need to write precisely without going off down "rabbit trails," then announce that for the next several days or weeks, they must cut their first drafts in half when they revise them yet must keep everything that was good about their first draft! Require your students to count the words in their first draft and divide by two. That becomes the maximum number of words they can have in their revised draft. How do they achieve this reduction without eliminating important information? Primarily by removing words, phrases, and sentences that don't significantly contribute to what they were trying to accomplish in the first draft, but also by replacing phrases and sentences with fewer words that more precisely say what they want to say.

This combination of revising by removing and revising by replacing, in order to sharpen what they have to say, makes students' writing sound more mature to them and to readers. In fact, there is probably no better mark of quality writing in middle and high school than precision and economy of expression.

What If?

What if Your Students Again Start Resisting Revision?

We expect many, if not most, students to resist revising their papers when we first begin teaching them how to do it—that's natural. However, by the various means we have discussed in this chapter, you can overcome that resistance in almost all cases. Sometimes, however, after an extended period of things going well, some students may again show resistance to revising their papers. There are three common reasons for this "backsliding."

Over the years, we have noticed that students can become disenchanted with revising, after doing it successfully for a while, when they are required to revise every first draft. To prevent this problem from occurring in the first place, or to eliminate it if it has already begun to reveal itself, give your students a choice of which first drafts they have to revise.

One of the most important pieces of equipment for any writer is a trash can! All writers have false starts and works they leave unfinished. Every writer has first drafts they feel good about, and first drafts they would just as soon forget. When students are required to revise every first draft, it is like saying that every first draft is worthy of publication. Students begin to dread working longer and harder on a piece they do not feel is worth the effort. Not only does having to revise every first draft soon begin to build new student resistance to revising, but if it continues it will soon build new student resistance to first draft writing as well.

Have your students write new first drafts regularly while you are teaching them how to revise. That way, they will always have at least three new first drafts to choose from each time they select one they want to work on to make it better.

Two other common reasons for renewed resistance to revising are related to each other. One of these is when students are expected to apply the same strategy in the same way too many times in a row; the other one is when students are taught to revise by replacing before they have learned to how to revise by adding. In other words, revision can be boring if you pace your instruction too slow or frustrating if

(continued)

you pace it too fast. To prevent or solve the frustration problem, notice which students are not able to do the particular application of the strategy you have been teaching. Meet with these students in a small group to give them extra help with it. To prevent or solve the boredom problem, rotate through the applications within the strategy you are teaching. For example, once you have taught students to revise by adding words or phrases and most students seem to be getting it, move to teaching revising by adding dialogue until most students seem to be getting it. Then, move to revising by adding a missing part until most students seem to be getting it. Next, however, rather than moving on to revising by replacing, return to adding words or phrases for a while, then to revising by adding dialogue, and so on. You will find that students will have much less problem with boredom this way than if you stay with revising by adding words or phrases until everyone learns it. Recycling multiple times through the different applications of a revising strategy before moving to a new revising strategy helps prevent both frustration and boredom.

Teaching Your Students to Revise While They Write

So far in this chapter, we have presented revising as something writers do when they look back at their writing. All published writers do revise after finishing a first draft, but they also revise as they write. Older children need to watch you revise as you write—particularly adding or replacing words or phrases. However, the need to remove or reorder, and the need for a better beginning or end, are often not apparent until a piece is finished. To model revising while writing, it is necessary that you do a lot of "thinking aloud" as you write during mini-lessons. Doing some simple revising as you write and thinking aloud to explain the reasons for your revisions will teach your students that you don't need to wait until you are finished writing to think about how to make it even better.

At the end of the writing time on some days, ask your students if anyone did any revising while they were writing and have volunteers tell what they revised and why. Before too long, you will see most of your children making small but important revisions as they write their first draft.

Depending on the age and writing sophistication of your students, you may want to teach only some of the four revising strategies—probably the easier ones of adding and replacing. Regardless of what you decide is appropriate to teach your students this year, you should post a chart to remind you and your students what they know about revising.

> ### Revising—Making your Writing EVEN Better
>
> Look again at your writing. Pick a friend to look with you.
>
> Use special revising pens or cut and tape.
>
> Add (Push in):
>
> > Words that make the writing more vivid or clearer
> >
> > Dialogue that makes the writing come alive
> >
> > Missing information
>
> Replace (Trade):
>
> > Boring words
> >
> > Telling with showing
> >
> > Beginnings that don't grab the readers' attention
> >
> > Endings that don't answer the readers' questions
>
> Remove (Chop out):
>
> > Sentences or paragraphs that don't stay on topic or distract the reader
>
> Reorder (Cut and sort):
>
> > Sentences or paragraphs that are not in the right sequence
>
> Revise while you are writing.

Three Reasons for Teaching Revision

One reason to teach students how to revise some of their papers is so these papers will be even better—that is, clearer, more interesting, more persuasive, more moving, or more complete. Certainly, this is the main reason all published writers revise. Even award-winning writers can and do significantly improve their writing when they revise it.

A second reason to require and help students revise some of their writing is so that, in time, they will eventually learn to revise while they write. Although no amount of revision while writing can replace the benefits of revising a completed draft, revising while writing does make first drafts better than they would otherwise be. Because not all writing that your students will do in the future can be revised in a separate revision step, they must learn to revise as they write so that they can eventually learn to produce adequate first drafts.

Moreover, a third reason for instruction in revision is because it teaches students how to write better. That is, students first learn to do things during a separate revision step that, in due course, they will be able to do automatically while writing. For example, as students learn to revise their beginnings by replacing them, you will gradually see an improvement in the beginnings of their first drafts. The time they spend focusing solely on improving the beginning of a complete draft eventually helps them know how to write better beginnings to start with. For another example, as your students learn to replace overused and inexact words with more varied and precise words during revision, you will gradually see an improvement in word choice in their first drafts. And this process has a never-ending benefit! Because writers never master beginnings or word choice or any other creative aspect of writing, they always have more to learn by focusing on a single aspect of a completed draft during a separate revision step.

Looking Back
Revision Matters!

To incorporate revision into your writing curriculum:

- Make sure your students know that revision is different from editing.
- Be enthusiastic about how revision can help your students write papers that are more understandable, more interesting, more persuasive, and so on.
- Teach your students that *all* successful writers revise and all published writing has been revised. We revise to make our good writing *even* better.
- Don't begin revision instruction until your students can edit their own papers with help from a basic editor's checklist.
- Once your students begin learning to revise, teach them to always revise before editing. Otherwise, they'll have to edit their papers twice!
- Use mini-lessons, conferences, and partners to teach each revising strategy, and support your students' application of that strategy to revise their own papers.
- Begin by teaching your students to revise by adding, then by replacing. Eventually, they can learn how to revise by reordering and by removing.
- Have your students write new first drafts regularly so they will have at least three new first drafts to choose from each time they are going to revise one.
- Teach your students to revise while they write.

Chapter 8

Revising across the Curriculum

Revision of first drafts makes them even better, gradually helps students learn to revise while writing, and eventually teaches them how to write better.

What a bonus it is that revision can also increase student learning of science, social studies, literature, and other school subjects! That's because, when students write about any topic, their papers reflect both their writing ability and their understanding of the topic. In the previous chapter, we explained how you can use revision to improve various aspects of your students' writing ability. In this chapter, we discuss how you can also use revision to enhance your students' learning across the curriculum.

Writing, Revising, and Learning across the Curriculum

One of the main reasons some students don't like to write, and others have trouble writing much or well, is the prior-knowledge problem. In order to write, we must write *about* something. We can't write well about what we don't know. We can't write well about what we don't understand. We can't write clearly and interestingly about anything unless we know the vocabulary. This is why it helps your students learn to write better when you have them write about what they are learning across the curriculum. It is a major way you can reduce your students' prior-knowledge problem in writing. Moreover, writing about what they are learning helps your students learn it better, especially when they revise some of what they have written.

Metaphorically speaking, all learning is revision. Whenever people (young and old) learn, they acquire new knowledge or attitudes, modify their existing knowledge or attitudes, discard some of what they previously believed or felt, or change some of the interrelationships among their beliefs and feelings. Since learning is revision of existing knowledge or attitudes, your students' revisions of some of their writing can boost their learning of whatever subject you are having them write about.

In Chapter 4, we discussed a variety of think-writes that help students learn more in every area of the curriculum by getting them to activate prior knowledge, make predictions, or construct brief summaries. Because think-writes are single-draft writing that students do for themselves, they do not need to be edited. And because think-writes are quick ways to facilitate thinking and learning of content, revision is unnecessary and could even be counterproductive.

In Chapter 6, we described how writing short pieces of various kinds can also facilitate student learning of subject matter. Since these pieces will be seen by classmates and possibly others, they need to be edited and thereby provide students with additional practice in proofreading and self-correction. However, these kinds of writing fulfill their function by being written, shared, and published, so there is no need for students to revise them.

In this chapter, we focus on the kinds of student writing across the curriculum we call *learning products*. A learning product is a demonstration in writing of each student's current knowledge or attitudes in some area of the curriculum. A written learning product provides you and your students with a snapshot of their present state of understanding that then serves as a concrete opportunity for them to learn more by revising that understanding. When you have your students compose a piece of writing that represents their learning to this point, their written product is a concrete stand-in for their learning. As they revise this piece of writing, they are revising their understanding at the same time. Therefore, revision is simultaneously helping them learn how to write better and increasing their learning in whatever subject you had them write about.

A written learning product can also be an opportunity for students to demonstrate or develop advanced thinking about what they are studying in your class. Although every subject in the curriculum has content for students to master, every subject also requires higher-level skills. For example, the study of literature not only teaches students information about authors and their works but it also teaches students how to interpret and critique literary pieces. Quizzes and tests can do a reasonable job of evaluating whether students have learned information, but they are notoriously weak in evaluating student ability to interpret, critique, or engage in other higher-level skills. Writing has long been the method of choice for teachers to determine whether students can employ higher-level skills to any domain they are studying. Consequently, revision of learning products written to demonstrate higher-level thinking is an important way to enhance those skills.

What If?

What if Students Resist Revision across the Curriculum?

Although what students revise in their papers often differs when they are writing about what they have been learning across the curriculum, the way you teach them to revise is the same. If students have not learned to revise before being asked to reread and rewrite a learning product about social studies, science, or other subject, many of them will either resist revising or will edit instead. All the means presented in the previous chapter for gradually overcoming this resistance are as necessary and as helpful when revising learning products as when revising writing in general. Mini-lessons are as important and necessary for revision across the curriculum as for personal writing. Motivation is at least as much of a challenge when students are writing about subject-matter learning as when they are doing self-selected writing.

There are two approaches you can take to guide revision across the curriculum. The first approach teaches student writers to apply the four general revising strategies from the previous chapter in ways that make their learning products better. The second approach teaches them to use writing scales to evaluate their own written learning products and direct how they revise them.

Applying the Four General Revising Strategies to Writing across the Curriculum

As with writing in general, students can revise their written learning products in science, social studies, literature, and so on, by adding, replacing, removing, or reordering. The particular applications of these four strategies when revising writing across the curriculum will vary, depending on the learning the writing was designed to facilitate or demonstrate.

Revising Written Learning Products by Adding (Pushing In)

Adding academic vocabulary. As soon as your students are willing and able to revise their first drafts by adding words or phrases, they are ready to learn to revise their written learning products across the curriculum by adding facts and comments containing subject-specific and unit-specific words and phrases. By doing so, they will have another, powerful opportunity to learn this academic vocabulary better.

Every subject across the curriculum has specialized vocabulary. Math has scores of terms, such as *subtract, denominator, polygon,* and *improper.* Science has *conductor, asteroid, habitats,* and many more. Social studies has *suburban, patriotism, peninsula,* and so on. Literature has *sonnet, metaphor, plot,* and many others. Terms such as *sportsmanship, percussion,* and *perspective* are part of the academic vocabulary in physical education, music, and art, respectively. An important part of what educators teach in any subject across the curriculum is that subject's core vocabulary

appropriate for the students' current grade level. Every student who is successfully learning math, science, social studies, literature, physical education, music, or art can speak and write using that subject's core vocabulary.

Imagine you are teaching a unit in social studies on the New England states. The first part of the unit has emphasized the geography of New England. Before you move on to the history of the region, you ask your students to write a summary of what they have learned so far. The next day, to increase what they have already learned about New England geography, you have them revise their summaries. Here is a mini-lesson from which your students could learn that adding some academic vocabulary to a learning product can make it more precise and read more like an "expert" wrote it:

> Boys and girls, last night I also wrote a short summary of what we have been studying so far in our unit on the New England states. I've made a transparency from my paper so you can help me make what I wrote even better. Read it to yourselves and then we'll talk about it. I want to make sure my paper reads like I know what I'm talking about!

If you have a vocabulary wall somewhere in your room where you display core geography terms and terms specific to your unit on the New England states, it will help tremendously. Otherwise, you may need to have your class brainstorm important words and phrases from the unit so far, so you can write them on the board before your mini-lesson.

In your written summary, you have purposefully avoided using much of the academic vocabulary you have been teaching in social studies this year or in your unit on the New England states. Here could be your summary, kept very brief so there is plenty of room for your students to help you add word, phrases, and facts:

> New England is in the north of the United States. There are six states in New England. Most of the states are close together. Five of the six states border on the ocean.

Explain that using more of the vocabulary you have been studying will help make your writing more exact. As you refer the class to the vocabulary wall or list of brainstormed terms on the board, take one sentence at a time and ask them what you could add so the sentence becomes more exact and sounds more like an expert wrote it. Occasionally, the students will probably suggest that you add a new sentence. Here is an example of some appropriate additions they could help you make that use more of the academic vocabulary from your unit so far.

> **east region**
> New England is in the north, of the United States. There are six
> **Rhode Island is not an island!**
> states in New England. Most of the states are close together. Five of
> **have a coast because they**   **Atlantic**   **Vermont is the only New**
> the six states, border on the, ocean. **England state that is landlocked.**

After you have revised your summary by adding these words, phrases, and facts, ask your students to quickly help you edit your revised draft. Someone should notice that *ocean* now needs to be spelled with a capital. If not, give them hints until one of the children suggest it. Draw a slash through the small *o* and write a capital *O* above it.

If your students are used to mini-lessons on revising and editing, it will not be necessary for you to take the time to copy your revised and edited summary over, but if you did, it might look like this:

> New England is in the northeast region of the United States. There are
>
> six states in New England. Most of the states are close together. Rhode
>
> Island is not an island! Five of the six states have a coast because they
>
> border on the Atlantic Ocean. Vermont is the only New England state that
>
> is landlocked.

Whether you have copied your revised and edited summary over or not, put another transparency with your original on the overhead so your students can compare your "before and after." Ask them which version is more exact and reads more like it was written by an expert.

Immediately after this mini-lesson, turn off the overhead projector and ask your students to take out the summaries you asked them to write the day before. Tell them you want them to revise their summaries the way they helped you revise yours by adding some terms from the vocabulary on the wall or board and any facts these words and phrases help them remember. Unless your students are quite used to revising, you will find it helpful to pair them up for a few minutes to confer before they begin revising by adding academic vocabulary. Each partner's job during this peer conference is to read the other's paper and make suggestions for additions using words and phrases from the board or vocabulary wall. As your students revise, walk around and encourage them. You will be pleased with the additional learning that is evidenced in their revised summaries, especially their ability to use academic vocabulary appropriately.

Adding Examples. Once your students are able to revise their learning products (and their learning!) by adding academic vocabulary and facts expressed using that vocabulary, there is another kind of revision by adding you may want to consider teaching them. One of the most important revisions that children can learn to make to their content writing and learning is to add examples. In math and literature learning products, especially, students often restate principles, rules, or generalizations you have taught them, but without examples to flesh them out.

Examples help readers understand better and they can show whether writers really know what they are talking about! Whenever we ask our students to summarize what they have learned about a topic or subtopic or to answer a question, it can help them to revise their written summaries or answers by looking for opportunities to add an example. We teach revision by adding examples in the same way we taught revision by adding academic vocabulary:

1. Have each student write a learning product based on what you have taught so far in one of your content units.

2. Write a brief one of these learning products of your own that needs but lacks examples.

3. Teach a revision mini-lesson during which your students help you add one or more examples to your learning product.

4. Partner your students up for a few minutes to help each other decide where and what examples to add.

5. Have your students revise their learning products by adding one or more examples.

For instance, imagine you have been teaching a poetry unit in literature. You have taught a poem each day and provided time for your students to work in book club groups sharing poems from books of poetry for children that you checked out of your school and public libraries. You have posted a chart in the room that gives the names and authors of the poems you taught as well as the three favorite poems selected by each book club group to share with the class as a whole. The emphasis in the unit has been on getting your students to enjoy reading and listening to poetry, but you have also spent some time teaching the poet's craft. At the end of the unit, you could decide to have your students write the answer to the question, "What are some features that poems often have?," or "How do poets make their poems enjoyable to read?," or even, "What are some differences between poetry and prose?," depending on the age and sophistication of your students. Chances are that few of these papers will include specific examples from the poems listed to support the students' answers. So, having them revise their papers by adding examples from those poems would not only be appropriate but it would also help your students learn to write with examples as well as understand the poet's craft even better. In addition, by rethinking and revisiting some of those poems to mine them for examples, your students would understand and appreciate them even better as well.

Why Not?

Why Not Teach Students to Write with Examples to Start with, Rather than Teaching Them to Add Them During Revision?

The writing process, including separate steps for revising and editing, is helpful to developing writers because it allows them to focus on one aspect of their papers at a time, rather than trying to keep everything in mind at the same time. As we demonstrated in the first three chapters of this book, the only way to overcome most students' lack of self-confidence, motivation, and independence in writing and to use writing to increase their learning and thinking is to emphasize those factors in the writing we ask them to do. By having students revise and edit some of what they write, we can also accomplish our instructional goals for teaching specific skills in writing or enhancing particular kinds of subject-matter learning, without making first drafts harder and less motivating for our students to write.

Revising Written Learning Products by Replacing (Trading)

Students who can revise by adding are ready to learn to revise by replacing. Replacing words or phrases, sentences, or chunks of text that are incomplete, are imprecise, or include incorrect information is an important means to help students compose better learning products, learn how to write better, and complete, hone, or correct learning across the curriculum.

Replacing words and phrases with academic vocabulary. In the same way, and for the same reason, that we taught our students to add subject-specific and unit-specific words and phrases to their writing across the curriculum, we teach them to replace everyday or imprecise terminology with academic vocabulary. The best way at this point is to combine the two kinds of revision so students now revise their written learning product both by adding academic vocabulary and facts expressed in that vocabulary, and by replacing common terms with more specialized ones. If your students only learn to revise their writing about subject matter in this way, it will be enough for you to notice significant progress in their writing and learning. Over time, you will see gradual improvements in your students' word choices in all the writing they do—an important skill. Your students will learn the academic vocabulary you teach them better, because they are focusing on it and using it to write. Your students will understand what you are teaching across the curriculum better because meaningful vocabulary knowledge is an important contributor to reading and language comprehension.

Other Kinds of Revision by Adding, Replacing, Reordering, or Removing

Most other additions or replacements you ask your students to make in a written learning product require them to work with a partner or to consult a source. In writing about topics from social studies, science, and other subjects, the emphasis is usually on the quantity and quality of the information in the paper. When writers are expected to revise their learning product other than by having more academic vocabulary or adding examples, they usually need more or better information before they can add it or use it to replace what they already have. Of course, a partner can read or listen to the paper and help the writer remember more of what you have taught in the unit they have written about. Generally, however, it facilitates these kinds of revisions more when the writer or the partners revisit a source or check a new one. The most straightforward way to do this is to require your students to write their learning product from memory, rather than allowing them to write with a textbook or other source open beside them, but allow them to use the textbook or other source during revision. Why? Because students will try to remember what you are teaching better when they know they may have to write about it from memory. Yet, by allowing them to revisit a source or consult a new one during revision, you are giving them another opportunity to learn information without undermining their motivation to learn it to start with.

Original

Our class went outside to the woods behind the school and dug a hole. We piled the dirt up so it looked like a little mountain. We took our 6 inch rulers and stuck them in 3 inches deep all around the mountain. Then, we took turns pouring water from a sprinkling can on top of the mountain. I observed that there were little streams going down the sides of the mountain. I observed that the dirt eroded around all the rulers.

Revision Version with Beginning and Ending Added after Using a Source

Erosion happens when solid parts of land are carried away by water, wind, or animals. Soil erosion is a problem for farmers all over the world.

Our class went outside to the woods behind the school and dug a hole. We piled the dirt up so it looked like a little mountain. We took our 6 inch rulers and stuck them in 3 inches deep all around the mountain. Then, we took turns pouring water from a sprinkling can on top of the mountain. I observed that there were little streams going down the sides of the mountain. I observed that the dirt eroded around all the rulers.

It would help prevent erosion if vegetation was growing on the sides of the mountain. Vegetation also helps prevent erosion in farm land.

Using Writing Scales to Self-Evaluate and Revise Writing across the Curriculum

The second approach you can take to guide revision across the curriculum teaches your students to use writing scales to evaluate their own written learning products and direct their revision of them. Whenever you expect your students to include specific facts or types of information in a written learning product or to write in a certain form, a writing scale is the most effective tool you can use to steer their rereading and rewriting.

What is a writing scale? It is a little like a writing rubric, but much simpler, so your students can learn to use it independently. A rubric takes account of every trait in a student's paper—as many as six or seven (ideas/content, conventions, voice, etc.); a scale usually focuses on only one trait. A rubric is generally designed to apply to different kinds of writing on any topic; a scale is used to help students to improve one kind of writing or even a single assignment. The criteria on a rubric tend to be fairly general, whereas the criteria on a writing scale are always specific. A rubric evaluates each component of the paper on a three-, four-, or five-point scale; a scale only has two evaluation points for each question it asks about the paper: yes or no. Because a rubric is used to assign an overall grade or score to the paper, the subscores for the different traits must be combined; a scale is not used to give the paper a grade or score, but to guide revision or editing so the paper gets all "yes" responses.

A writing scale is a list of two or more yes/no criteria or questions that students ask about their own first drafts. It focuses their attention on some essential parts of the content or form of what they have written to guide their self-evaluation, revision, or editing. For example, an editor's checklist is one type of writing scale. In this section, we discuss writing scales that can help students revise their writing across the curriculum.

Information Checklists

The simplest scale for evaluating and revising writing across the curriculum is an information checklist. This kind of writing scale is a list of facts, characteristics, or other items you would like your students' papers to include. They use this checklist alone or in partners to self-evaluate the content of their first draft, then revise it by adding items they don't have and replacing words or items they have but that are incorrect or incomplete in some way.

Because you do not want unmotivated writers or boring and awkwardly worded first drafts, you wait to show your students the information checklist until they have written their learning product. You answer any questions they have about particular items on the scale, and then you display your first draft so they can help you check it for the information on the list. Ideally, you will have to add one or two items of information to your draft, but it is also important that you replace at least one item you have with one that is more accurate or complete. Be aware that students are often quite literal with an information checklist. Even if they have said the same thing as an item on the checklist but in different words, they will sometimes want to replace their wording with the one on the checklist. You won't be able to prevent this entirely, but do try. One way to reduce this tendency is to model during your mini-lesson giving yourself a check on the scale for items you have correct but worded differently. Reading it aloud the way you have it and the way it is worded on the checklist and asking students whether they think the two mean the same thing is a good way to proceed through your draft. When they mean the same thing, give yourself a check; when they do not, revise your draft by replacing your wording with wording that does mean the same thing. This teaches them the process they need to follow in their heads when they use the list to check and revise their own papers.

Imagine you have read the first two *Little House on the Prairie* books by Laura Ingalls Wilder to your class this year and that several of your students have read other of those books. Recently, you brought an LCD projector into your room that you connected to a laptop computer with a wireless Internet connection. You showed your class several websites that you had bookmarked in advance to teach them about Laura's life after the stories in the first two books, especially the later years when she was writing the series. You decided to culminate your author study of Wilder by having your students write a biography of her. You constructed the following information checklist for them to use as a writing scale to self-evaluate and revise their biographies:

Information Checklist for the Laura Ingalls Wilder Biography

She was born in Wisconsin in 1867.

Her parents were Charles and Caroline Ingalls.

She married Almanzo Wilder when she was 18.

She taught in a one-room school when she was 15.

She and Almanzo had one daughter, who became the writer Rose Wilder Lane.

She published the first *Little House* book when she was 65.

Her daughter may have helped her write the books.

Laura died in Missouri in 1957 when she was 90.

It will be an unusual student whose first draft has all this information included correctly. Yet, it is important to notice that the best biographies your students write will include more personal and interesting information than just the items on your checklist. Had you given your students this checklist before they wrote, the biographies they produced would have been much more similar, been worded much more like the checklist items, and would have had much less of the other information that makes them interesting to write, share, and read. And, they would have been more boring to write!

Information checklists are appropriate for a wide range of writing across the curriculum. Using an information checklist to guide student revision is an effective way of ensuring that your students get the essential information correct in a particular piece of writing without thwarting their interest, creativity, or initiative.

What If?

What if Students Revise by Inserting Sentences Verbatim from the Information Checklist?

Unpack the sentences into facts or phrases that must be combined with other information by the students to make sentences. For example, the first sentence on the Laura Ingalls Wilder checklist would become:

> Born in Wisconsin
>
> Born in 1867

Simply adding by copying will no longer work!

Using Writing Scales to Teach Narrative, Descriptive, Expository, and Persuasive Writing

One of the goals of writing instruction at certain grade levels, depending on where you live, is to teach students how to produce one or more of the "four modes" of writing: narrative, descriptive, expository, and persuasive. These modes are really "super-genres" that have been so broadly defined that almost any piece of prose can be classified as an example of one of the four. Of course, any and all of these modes can be taught to students during personal or other writing. However, we believe they are best taught during writing across the curriculum. Here's why.

Earlier in this chapter, we cited the lack of prior knowledge as one of the main reasons some students write little or poorly. The prior-knowledge problem is even greater when the purpose for the writing you ask your students to do emphasizes the form. If your students lack prior knowledge when the writing is topic driven, any efforts they expend trying to remember information or gain information from you, their partner, or other sources requires extra motivation, but the results are worth it. However, when the writing they are to do is form driven, any effort they expend to remember or gain information about the topic distracts them from their purpose for writing. This means that when you are teaching your students how to write one of these four modes, you want them to write on a topic they already know as much about as possible. Only then will they be free to concentrate on how they write about the topic rather than the topic itself.

It is effective to teach students how to write one or more of the four modes by having them write about what have learned across the curriculum because it helps them overcome the prior-knowledge problem, but that is not the only reason. Each of the modes exists because each mirrors different ways to think about a subject. For example, when you ask students to write expository papers on science topics that are organized by a cause-and-effect pattern, you help them learn to think in a way that is close to the very essence of science—how things in nature work the way they do.

Characteristics of the Four Modes

When teaching any or all of the four modes, it helps if you understand what most distinguishes each from the others. First, it is important to note that the name of the mode (narrative, descriptive, expository, persuasive) refers to the text as a whole that is being labeled. So, when we say that a student's paper is a narrative, we mean it is a narrative overall, even though it may contain a section that is descriptive or some other mode if we look at it by itself.

Second, two structural characteristics generally enable you to classify a student's paper or other piece of prose as belonging to one of the four modes: the nature of the subject and the organizational pattern of the ideas. The *subject* is the single-most important thing the paper is about. The *organizational pattern* is the way the ideas in the paper are arranged relative to each other.

Mode	Nature of the Subject	Organizational Pattern
Narrative	A character or person A place An event	Chronological sequence
Descriptive	A character or person A place An object A feeling	Set(s) of characteristics, many of which are sensory
Expository	[One or more subjects of any kind]	Logical sequence Explanation Question and answer Problem and solution Cause and effect or Compare and contrast
Persuasive	An opinion	Reasons with their supports

Obviously, *expository writing* is really a catchall term for at least six different kinds of writing, each of which must be learned when it is suitable for students to do so. Fortunately, the other three modes have much less variation within them.

Many writing assignments, though not all, implicitly or explicitly call for one of the four modes. For example, when you ask students to write a biography or summarize the life of a person your class has been studying, you expect them to write a narrative with the person as the subject and organized in chronological sequence. Even if a student uses flashbacks or flash-forwards when writing the paper, the organizing principle of the student's *ideas* in the paper will still be chronological. For another example, when you ask your students to write how two particular states in the United States are the same and how they are different, you expect them to write an expository paper with the two states as the subject and organized as a comparison–contrast. In both of these examples, a student who merely describes the person's life by listing randomly ordered events and achievements, or each state by listing its characteristics, has not written in the most appropriate mode for the assignment. For a third example, when you ask your students to discuss the conflict in a story they have read in their literature anthology, you expect them to write an exposition with the conflict as the subject and organized as a problem and solution, rather than a narrative.

Using Graphic Organizers to Plan the Organization of a Paper

In Chapter 2, we pointed out that graphic organizers can help students plan before writing. When we are teaching students to write one or more of the four modes, they become even more helpful, if not essential. The hardest kind of revision a student can undertake is to change the first draft's overall organizational pattern. It is generally easier to start the paper over from scratch. Therefore, we use graphic organizers, especially when teaching expository writing, to help students plan their writing so they are more likely to organize their papers in the most appropriate way to start with. Then, a writing scale can help them tweak and flesh out their organization, without requiring them to change it to an entirely new pattern. Fortunately, each of the major organizational patterns in the four modes can be visually represented by one or more kinds of graphic organizers:

Organization	*Graphic Organizers*
Chronological sequence	Time line
Set(s) of characteristics	List Cluster Semantic feature matrix Data chart
Logical sequence	Time line Step-by-step table or chart
Explanation	Web Outline
Question and answer Problem and solution	Two-column chart

Organization	Graphic Organizers
Cause and effect	Two-column chart Cause-and-effect chain
Compare and contrast	Venn diagram/Double Bubble Semantic feature matrix Data chart
Reasons with their supports	Web Outline

By combining an appropriate graphic organizer for planning the first draft with a writing scale to guide self-evaluation and revision, we can gradually and eventually teach all our students to produce acceptable examples of each of the four modes.

Developing a Writing Scale for Narrative, Descriptive, or Persuasive Writing

The first criterion or question on a writing scale for self-evaluating and revising writing in one of these three modes should help students learn to write to the assignment:

1. Does the paper have the topic that was assigned?

The second criterion or question on a writing scale for these modes should deal with the unity of the writing. Every kind of writing has a subject that should be maintained throughout the piece—something that many children have trouble with. Here are second questions that get at the unity of the piece that students can be taught to answer about each of three modes:

2. Is the paper clearly about just one character, person, place, or event? [narrative writing]

2. Is the paper clearly about just one character, person, place, object, or feeling? [descriptive writing]

2. Is the paper clearly arguing for just one opinion? [persuasive writing]

If your students are beginning to learn how to write one of these three modes, you may choose to start your writing scale for that mode with just the first two questions. When your students are able to produce first drafts that consistently allow their readers to be able to answer *yes* to both of these questions, they have learned how to write to the assignment and maintain unity of subject—both very important writing skills. Then you can choose to move to another mode or add third and fourth criteria to your scale for the same mode.

The trickiest part of developing a writing scale for these three modes is formulating questions that get at the basic structure of ideas in that form. Here are possible third and fourth questions for each of the three modes:

3. Does the paper tell exactly what happened? [narrative]

3. Does the paper give many details of the person, place, thing, or feeling it is about? [descriptive]

3. Are there at least three different reasons given to support the opinion? [persuasive]

4. Is it clear what happened first, what happened after that, and what happened last? [narrative]

4. Are the details expressed in language that helps the reader imagine what they look, smell, sound, taste, or feel like? [descriptive]

4. Is each reason supported with facts, evidence, examples, or arguments? [persuasive]

Finally, every writing scale needs to have some questions that get students to self-evaluate how well they execute the organization pattern they planned using a graphic organizer. We can use the same three questions for all three modes:

5. Does the paper have a good beginning, or does it "start in the middle"?

6. Does the paper have a good ending, or does it "leave us hanging"?

7. Does each sentence nicely connect to the next one, or do we sometimes have to say "huh?"

Our writing scale for narrative, descriptive, or persuasive writing would consist of the corresponding seven questions for that mode.

Developing Writing Scales for Expository Writing

Because there are at least six kinds of expository writing, depending on how the ideas are organized, it is probably not a good idea to think of it as a single mode, but as a mixed bag of ways to analyze topics in writing. In fact, if a piece of writing is prose, but not clearly narrative, descriptive, or persuasive, then it is expository by default. Of course, that may help us classify pieces correctly as expository, but it does nothing to help anyone learn to write them!

It is probably essential to provide students with an appropriate graphic organizer and insist they use it to plan their first draft whenever we ask them to write in the expository mode. The writing scale we use to guide their revision can have the same question 1 and questions 5, 6, and 7 as the scales for the other three modes. However, questions 2, 3, and 4 will vary depending on the particular kind of expository writing the assignment calls for. For example, when we ask students to write a piece that requires them to compare and contrast two of something, the scale could have these questions:

2. Is the paper clearly about two things?

3. Does the paper have a section that tells us how the two things are alike?

4. Does the paper have a section that tells us how the two things are different?

Revising Learning Products to Teach Subject-Specific Writing Forms

Part of what it means for students to know a subject well is that they are able to talk and write about it in the way that experts do. That is, if a person really understands science, that person will not only use the terminology of science when talking or writing about it but will also be able to write about science in the forms that successful students of science are expected to produce as they progress up through the grades. Each subject in the curriculum has forms of writing that experts gradually learn how to produce. Written learning products are obviously the best place for students to demonstrate their acquisition of these forms. Revision of written learning products provides another opportunity for students to learn the forms of writing across the curriculum.

What is required is that you know the characteristics, components, and rules for the subject-specific form you want your students to learn how to write. In other words, what criteria will you look at to evaluate their attempts to produce the form? Some of those criteria become the questions you teach them to ask themselves about their paper during revision.

Looking Back
Revising across the Curriculum

Like revision in general, revision across the curriculum helps students learn to write better, but it also gives them an opportunity to increase their learning of science, social studies, math, and other school subjects.

- Many students will learn to write and revise better when they write about what they are learning in subject areas because they have learned lots of knowledge that they can share.

- Because all learning is revision, revising some of their written learning products is a way to help them learn by revising their current knowledge and attitudes.

- Students are as likely to resist revising across the curriculum as they are in any other kind of writing they do, but effective mini-lessons and maintaining a concern for student motivation in the ways we have them write and revise can overcome resistance.

- One approach to guiding revision across the curriculum is teaching students to apply the four general revising strategies in ways that make their learning products better.

- Another approach teaches them to use writing scales to evaluate and revise their own written learning products.

Chapter 9

Sharing and Publishing

To get all your students off to a successful start in writing in your classroom, we suggested that you begin your school year by defining writing as putting down on paper what you want to tell.

In mini-lessons, you wrote about things you wanted to tell your students and encouraged them to write about things they wanted to tell. As they wrote, you encouraged them to write what they wanted to tell—not just what they could spell—and you applauded when they used vivid words they had to spell as best they could instead of the more common words they could spell.

The idea that writing is telling put on paper requires that writers have an opportunity to share their writing with others. At the beginning of the year, this sharing is quite informal. You circle your students at the end of the writing time and let volunteers share. You model positive comments and questions that show your interest in the ideas the writer shared. You let each writer who shares call on a friend to make a comment or ask a question. You also demonstrate that you appreciate the various topics your students choose to write about by adding some ideas to your *Things I Might Write About List,* and you encourage your students to add to their personal topics list when someone shares an idea they would like to write about.

Sharing is critical to a successful writing program because it authenticates the idea that the major purpose of writing is to communicate your ideas to others. Sharing also demonstrates that the writing students do is not just for the teacher. In classrooms in which sharing is how each writing session is closed, students begin to write for an audience that is important to them—their friends and classmates. Even students who don't particularly like to write usually like to talk, and they soon see that getting some ideas down on paper is their ticket to talk. When you include a daily sharing time, all your students are more motivated to write because kids are social beings and writing leads to social interaction with their friends.

Publishing is another kind of sharing. Students publish some of their writing so that others can read it. Writing they publish, unlike writing they orally share, needs to be edited—and sometimes revised—so that others can easily read it. Before students publish, they conference with a trusted friend and with the teacher to make their writing as clear, interesting, and easy to read as possible. In this chapter, we will share with you a variety of formats that will make sharing and publishing a regular and do-able part of your classroom routine.

🦋 Sharing

Early in the year, you will find that circling your students and letting volunteers share is an easy and natural way to finish each writing session. As the year goes on, you may want to add some variety to your daily sharing. Here are some possibilities.

Pair and Share

Pair and Share is a quick alternative to whole-class sharing. If you have your students seated in talking partners, they can just share with their partners. A quick alternative that gets different children paired up each time you do it is to shuffle a deck of index cards on which you have written each child's name. The first two cards that come out go to a designated spot in your room. The next two go to a second spot, and so on, until all your students are with their sharing partners for that day. Each partner then reads his or her piece. The listener's job is to make a positive comment and ask a question. The students then switch roles and the second child reads and the first child responds.

While your students are sharing, move around the room and listen in on some of the sharing pairs. Make a few notes about who wrote what and any particularly vivid words you heard. When the sharing time is over, make just a few positive comments about what you heard so your students know you are still interested in and appreciative of what they are writing.

> Some of you had some very interesting topics today. Ian told about his cat having kittens. You may want to ask him to tell you about that. Deagan added on to the story he started yesterday and it is getting very interesting. Erin wrote about how her bus got a flat tire on the way to school this morning. That's why she was late! Josh wrote about his favorite television show and I am going to add that topic to my writing list because I have a favorite TV show too! I also heard some great words. David described his camping trip as *awesome* and Adam used the word *victorious* when he was writing about his favorite team in the basketball tournament.

These comments you make should not take more than a minute but they demonstrate to your students that you continue to be intrigued with their topics and impressed by their word choice. They also set up some social interaction spurred by writing which will likely continue during lunch and recess.

Pair and Share is an easy and fun alternative way of sharing. If you use the index card shuffling to determine the pairs, your students will share with lots of their classmates. Shy children who may not choose to share with the whole group are very comfortable sharing with just one other person. To get Pair and Share started successfully in your classroom, you will want to model the procedures a few times—choosing one child as your sharing partner and letting all your students listen in. You may also want to post a chart, reminding your students of their jobs as sharing partners and where the partners meet.

Pair and Share

1. Go quickly to your spot:

   1st pair: beanbag   7th pair: computer

   2nd pair: rocking chair   8th pair: sink

   3rd pair: bookcase   9th pair: word wall

   4th pair: back table   10th pair: back left corner

   5th pair: gerbil cage   11th pair: back right corner

   6th pair: teacher desk

2. First alphabetical name reads first.

3. Partner listens and responds:

       I like . . .

       I wonder . . . ?

4. Second alphabetical name reads next.

5. Partner listens and responds:

       I like . . .

       I wonder . . . ?

Small Group Sharing

This sharing alternative works like Pair and Share but the children are divided into small groups of three or four students. To achieve a different mix of children each time you do this, use the index cards with the names. The first four names form a group and go to spot 1. The first name called for each group is designated as the teacher and makes sure that everyone follows the "nice comments or questions only" procedures. The teacher in each group shares first and then the other children share in alphabetical order by first names. Just as with Pair and Share, you should circulate and make notes of a few comments you want to share about the topics and word choice. This sharing alternative works especially well with older children who care deeply about the responses of their peers. It will probably work more smoothly if students have already participated in Pair and Share and know the routines and expectations.

Author's Chair

As the year goes on and you begin publishing, you may want to use an Author's Chair procedure for your sharing. Divide your students into five groups and set up a rotation schedule so that each group shares every fifth day. Spread out your struggling and wonderful writers across the days so that each day you have a balance of students sharing. Daily, schedule the struggling writers to share first and do a quick rehearsal with those writers before they share their writing.

Author's Chair Schedule				
Day 1	**Day 2**	**Day 3**	**Day 4**	**Day 5**
Ian	Darius	Maria	Paolo	Kristin
Raffi	Rameesh	Carlos	Kelly	Joshua
Erin	Carlos	Tran	Michael	Kevin
Deagan	Jennifer	Tracy	Kate	Luke
Liz	Amy	Adam		

On their day, the children can share something they have written since their last sharing day. The writing shared in the Author's Chair does not have to be a published piece that has been revised, edited, and published. The writing may be a first draft, finished or unfinished, or a final product. After each writer reads the chosen piece, he or she calls on two friends to make comments or ask questions. Just as with other types of sharing, only positive comments are allowed.

This is a time when the children can listen to what their classmates are writing about, *think* about what they are saying or trying to say, and learn to respond to the writing appropriately. Comments let children know what they have done well; questions help them know what they left out or could say better when revising. When a student reads a piece that is not published, the focus of the Author's Chair is on what the classmates liked and what they would like to know more about. Answers to these questions might make the writing clearer or better. Questions could lead to revisions during the writing period the next day.

Author's Chair as a way of sharing got its name from the special chair you select. The Author's Chair can be just a student's chair placed in the front of the classroom, but more often it is a special stool, chair, or rocking chair. Some teachers buy an inexpensive plastic lawn chair and decorate it with paint, glitter, and write "Share Chair" or "Author's Chair" in attractive, bright, florescent letters on the back.

Conferencing

Conferencing is a special kind of sharing in which your students share their writing with you, their teacher. Conferencing with individual students about their writing is your chance to differentiate your instruction and give each writer the advice and assistance he or she needs to move forward. Writing conferences can take many forms but probably the most common is a conference in which you help a student get a piece ready for publication. If the piece being published is a short piece like those described in Chapter 5, your major job in the conference is to be editor-in-chief, checking that the spelling, mechanics, and usage are correct, and making the piece easy for the reader to read. Before doing an editing conference with a student, be sure that the student has worked with a friend to

edit for whatever items you have on the checklist. Begin your conference by complimenting each student on his or her ideas.

> I really like your word choice in this poem. Your vivid words paint pictures in my mind.
>
> You were very specific about what you liked about the concert. I am sure the band member who gets your thank-you note will appreciate knowing exactly what you liked.
>
> These are some excellent word problems. I think your classmates will enjoy solving them tomorrow.

Next, comment to each child on how well he or she edited for the items on the checklist. If the writer has some errors that relate to the editor's checklist items and should have been corrected in the partner editing, work with the child to fix those errors first.

> You and your partner did a good job of editing for the items on the checklist. I think we need to look at this sentence, however. Number 4 on our checklist says that names need capital letters. Do you see a name in this sentence that needs a capital letter? Good, change the first letter to a cap.

Finally, let the writer watch as you supply the correct spelling for circled words and correct any errors not on the checklist.

> I am so glad you used such vivid words and you did a good job of putting down letters for the sounds you heard. I am going to write the correct spelling for these words you circled above them so you can have them spelled correctly when you write your final copy of this thank-you note.
>
> There are a few other things you need to fix when you make your final copy. We haven't put these on the checklist yet but you need to fix them so your note is easy to read. You need to put commas between *drums, cymbals, and triangle*. Commas are how we separate words in a series to make them easy to read. In your last sentence, you wrote that all the songs was good and you need to change *was* to *were* so that it sounds right to the person you are sending the note to. A very nice thank-you note! Pick a notecard you like and copy your draft on it. Check each sentence as you write it to be sure you made all the corrections on your draft copy.

For some pieces, you will want your students to make some revisions before they edit and publish a piece. In this case, you will need to hold two conferences with each student. During the first conference, focus solely on the meaning of the piece and ignore any spelling, usage, or mechanics errors. Ignoring those errors is not easy but keep reminding yourself that you will tackle the "fixing" task once you and the writer are happy with the content and word choice of the piece. Just as in an editing conference, your first response in a revising conference should be to compliment some aspect of your student's writing.

> This is a hilarious description of what happened at your birthday party when the lights went out.
>
> I am so glad you chose this story to publish. I remember really liking it when you read it during our sharing time.
>
> This will make a great book on dolphins. It is jam-packed with interesting facts.

Next, suggest one change—addition, replacement, reordering—that the writer might make that would make the piece even better and move that writer forward in his or her writing development.

> You know what I think would make this piece even better? What if you added some dialogue—the words you heard your friends shout when the lights went out?
>
> This is a great story once I got into it but your beginning didn't really grab my attention. What if you take this event that happened in the middle and begin with it and then work backwards? Starting in the middle of things is one way writers grab the reader's attention immediately.
>
> You know what I wonder? I wonder about how long dolphins live? I have heard they live a very long time but I am not sure that is true. Do you think you could do a little research and find out what their average life span is—and maybe how old the oldest living dolphin is?

Once the child has made the revision you suggested, you should probably take a quick look at that and then send the child to edit with a friend for the items on the checklist and come back to you for an editing conference.

Publishing

What comes to mind when you think about your students publishing their writing? Do you conjure up images of the yearly Young Authors' Fair and cringe as you remember working late to get all those books published by the deadline? What is your attitude toward publishing in your classroom? What is the attitude of your students toward publishing? In many classrooms, publishing is narrowly defined as the perfectly written and illustrated book. Helping children create some books is a valid and valuable way of publishing but if you broaden your definition of publishing, you will discover many publishing options that can fit comfortably into your classroom routines.

Begin to expand your options by considering the meaning of the word *publish*. *Publish* and *public* both come from the Latin word for people. When something is public, it is available to the people. Literally to publish something means to make that thing public—available for people to read. This is the definition of publish we have been using throughout this book. Remember that in Chapters 1 and 4, we talked about starting the year with single draft-writing—writing that did not need to be edited or revised because the writing was not going to be read by anyone besides the writer. As the year goes on, however, and your students are writing more willingly and understand that writing is putting down what you want to tell—not just what you can spell—you teach them some basic editing and revising strategies. Anytime your students produce something that others are going to read, they are publishing—making public—their writing. Publishing matters because it is the only authentic reason for editing and revising. Not all writing can or should be published, but it is important in every classroom for children to publish some of their writing. If nothing is ever published, your students will always be writing for you—their teacher—or, in the case of think-writes, for themselves. Unless you publish, the revising and editing steps are meaningless drills. When you publish, you revise to make your writing more interesting, captivating, informative, or persuasive to your reader. You edit to make your writing easier for your readers to read. When you publish, you are thinking about who will read it. The people who will read it are your audience and only through thinking about your audience can writers develop their voice. Here are some common publishing options to consider using in your classroom.

Postcards, Notes, and Letters

In Chapter 6, suggestions were made for having your students write postcards, notes, and letters. Because these communications were written to be read by others, they needed to be edited. Students work in partners to edit for the items on the

Editor's Checklist and then you put on your editor-in-chief hat and do a final edit, helping each child to fix spelling, mechanics, and usage errors. Many teachers take their students through these steps with various types of communication and don't even realize that this counts as publishing. Publishing means making your writing public—for someone else to read—and that is exactly what happens with post-cards, notes, and letters. Consider beginning your publishing with these short communications. Students understand the need to edit and copy them and you can get them published with little stress or frenzy!

Class Books

Class books are commonly published in primary classrooms but they are a versatile publishing option in upper grades too, particularly if you connect them to your science and social studies units. In Chapter 6, we described three poetry formats—cinquains, Important Poems, and What's New? Children wrote cinquains about the weather, Important Poems about famous Americans and What's New? poems about mammals. After the poems are written, peer-edited, and edited by the editor-in-chief, your students could copy—or type—their poems and illustrate them with their own drawings or images downloaded from the Web. Bind them together in some way. Have one of your artistic students create a front and back cover. Voila! You have published a book—a book in which all your students are published authors.

Think about all the opportunities you have for producing class books across the curriculum and across your school year. If you are teaching first or second grade, your students might all contribute to a *What We Are Thankful For* book as Thanksgiving approaches. Older students might enjoy creating a class cookbook of *Our Favorite Thanksgiving Recipes*. Thanksgiving cinquains are fun for students of all ages.

The Important Poem and What's New? formats can be used regularly to review information from your units. Another option for reviewing information learned is to have your students make a class alphabet book related to a topic. Brainstorm all the possible key words that begin with each letter and assign each student to complete one or two pages for each letter. For younger students, the page may just contain a sentence or two.

B is for baboons, bears, and bats.

C is for cats, chipmunks, chimps, and cheetahs.

Older students can write several sentences trying to use as many words that begin with the letter and still write some sensible text.

B is for baboons, bears, and beavers.

Baboons are the biggest monkeys and eat bark, berries, and birds.

Bears can be brown or black and eat berries and beavers.

Beavers are brown mammals with broad tails who build dams.

Once you and your class begin publishing class books, you will discover infinite possibilities. Class books in which each student contributes a page are a publishing option you and your students will look forward to and take pride in.

Class Newspapers, Newsletters, and Websites

As technological advances begin to make their way into classrooms, more and more teachers are having their students publish some of their work in a class newspaper, in a newsletter, or on a website. Search the Web and you will find a wide variety of free and inexpensive publishing and website development software as well as lots of examples of publishing by classrooms just like yours. On the Microsoft website, you will find a simple template for a newsletter along with lots of practical suggestions for publishing your classroom newsletter. (This site also contains templates for many other publishing modes, including calendars, letters, notes, and postcards!) Proteacher is another site that has lots of practical ideas for newsletters and websites, including the very sensible idea that you communicate with as many parents as possible through your class website, and print out copies of the website whenever it is updated to send home to parents without Internet access. This idea saves paper and provides access for everyone. If you have children whose parents are not fluent in English, consider seeking out volunteers who will translate the newsletter so that all parents can feel involved and "in the loop."

The student writing you choose to publish in a newspaper, in a newsletter, or on a website will vary with the time of year, the age of your students, and the availability of some volunteer help. If you have created a classbook with some edited short pieces such as cinquains, Important Poems, and What's New? poems, you could also include these pieces on your newsletter website. This gives your students another opportunity to share the information learned and the writing of their classmates with parents, grandparents and other proud family members. Alternatively, you could publish these pieces only in the newspaper/newsletter/website and not create the class book.

Not everyone has to publish a piece in every newsletter or website. If you publish or update every week, you may want to set up a schedule in which a quarter or a third of your class publishes each week. You can accomplish this easily by dividing your class into thirds or quarters—including one of your most struggling and advanced writers in each publishing group. While the students who will publish in subsequent weeks work on first drafts, devote your time and energy to helping the publishing group revise and edit. Here is a possible publishing schedule you might follow to have six or seven of your students each week produce a piece for your newspaper/newsletter or website.

Monday   Have each child who will publish this week pick one piece from the first drafts in his writing folder or notebook. Meet with group to revise. Have each student read the chosen piece and call on group members to suggest one revision—addition, replacement, reordering or removing—to make the piece *even* better. Alternatively, have students work in revising partners. Choose the most struggling writer for your partner.

Tuesday   Let students make whatever revisions they choose based on Monday's revising sharing. Check their revisions and make additional suggestions if necessary.

Wednesday   Pair students of similar writing ability to edit for the items on your Editor's Checklist. Hold an editing conference with your most struggling writer.

Thursday   Hold individual editing conferences with students who edited in partners yesterday. Give the final OK on each piece. While you are holding editing conferences, have your students find or create an illustration to go with their pieces.

Friday   Get pieces typed into publishing program—by volunteers, older students or your writers if they are able. Scan and add illustrations.

If you teach in the upper elementary grades, consider having your students take over the production of the class newspaper/newsletter/website. This usually works best in the spring of the year when your students have been writing all year and have learned some editing and revising strategies.

Publishing Individual Books

Finally, we get to what most teachers think of as publishing—children writing, illustrating, and creating their own individual books. This is a perfectly legitimate way to publish in a classroom and you should probably do it at least once or twice across the year. We left it to last, however, because we want you to consider all the other publishing possibilities. When publishing individual books, the KISS rule—Keep It Super Simple—is the rule to live by. The books don't have to be grand productions with elaborate illustrations and permanently bound. Producing these elaborate books takes an inordinate amount of teacher and student time—time that does not contribute to the writing development of your students.

As you plan for your students to publish some individual books, you might consider the same kind of schedule suggested for having student produce individual pieces for your class newspaper, newsletter, or website. Six or seven of your students might publish each week. On the first day, you meet with the students and they get revising suggestions either from the group as a whole or from a revising partner of similar writing ability. After they make revisions, which you check, they edit with that same partner and then you do a final editor-in-chief edit. You may want them to copy the piece into a book—or if you have volunteer help, have the volunteer type the edited pages. If you can get volunteers to type the final product, don't feel guilty about not having the child copy the final product. Little is to be learned from copying—and many children make the same—or new mistakes in the process. The students should then do the illustrations and/or use some stamps or free clip art available on multiple websites. In general, the revising, editing, and book producing should not take more than a week. If you have your students on a schedule that has them publishing every third or fourth week, they will spend the majority of their time writing first drafts—which is where most of the writing growth and learning will occur.

Depending on the age of your students and their writing independence, you may want your students to publish on an "as ready" schedule. Rather than dividing the class into publishing groups, you might have students sign up when they are ready to publish. In most classrooms, students must have three or four good first drafts before they can choose one to publish. They bring the draft they want to publish to you and have a revising conference. You may also want them to select a friend or two who will read the piece with them and make suggestions for making the piece even better. Once they make and you approve the revisions, they edit with a partner for the items on the checklist and then bring the piece to you for a final edit.

As with newsletters and websites, there are many free and inexpensive software programs that will help you and your students publish individual books. *Easybook Deluxe* by Sunburst and *Storybook Weaver Deluxe* by Riverdeep are two excellent programs that will motivate you and your students to publish books that will make you and your students proud.

What If?

What if Some of My Students Never Publish Books?

Although publishing is not the most important part of writing, students do take a great deal of pride in the books they publish. Having a published book with the child's name on the author page sends a clear message to the author. "I can write. I am an author. I published this book." Conversely, if all the other students are publishing books and your struggling students are not, there is also a clear—if unintended—message there. "I am not a good writer. Everyone else is an author. I hate to write." If you decide to have your students publish individual books, commit yourself to having every student publish at least one book. In the following chapter, you will find suggestions for helping students publish when their writing skills lag way behind those of the rest of the class.

Looking Back

Sharing and Publishing

If you want your students to view writing as a way to tell about ideas and events they care about, sharing is essential. Publishing is one kind of sharing. When students publish a piece, they are making it public—for someone else to read. Revising and editing are required for publishing so that the writing is as clear, interesting, and easy to read as possible. To make sharing and publishing a regular part of your classroom routine:

- Begin the year by circling your students while letting volunteers share. Model positive comments and sincere questions and allow the writer to call on a few friends to make comments and ask questions.

- As the year goes on and students are writing longer pieces, use Pair and Share, small-group share, and Author's Chair to provide more in-depth opportunities for writers to share.

- As students begin to publish, use the time while students are writing to hold revising and editing conferences with individual writers.

- Before conferencing with you, make sure that your students conference with a partner for the items on the editor's checklist.

- Vary the way students publish and make sure that publishing is not taking too much time and energy away from writing.

Chapter 10

Writing Interventions

Even if most of your students are making good progress in writing, you will have some students who require extra support if they are going to reach their writing potential.

Because writing is complex, there are many factors that can result in some of your students deciding that they are not good writers. Some children don't consider themselves good writers because of the way their papers look. Handwriting may be barely legible and there may be numerous spelling, mechanical, and usage errors. Many struggling writers call everything they write a "story" and have no notion about different writing forms and genres. Many children are poor writers because they have a "once and done" approach to writing. Once they finish writing, they consider the piece done and have neither the strategies nor the inclination to revise or edit. Some children have physical disabilities that make it very difficult for them to write using pencil and paper. Children who are learning English face some special challenges in writing. Specifically, vocabulary and syntax are almost universal problems for children learning to write as they learn a new language. In this chapter, we will describe some interventions for some of the most common writing difficulties faced by writers.

For your students who find writing particularly difficult, observe them as they write and look at their writing. Ask yourself: "What seems to cause them the greatest difficulty?" Children who don't write well usually have many problems but trying to deal with all the issues at once will probably not get you or them anywhere. What *one problem* could you tackle that would visibly improve their writing? Tackle that problem and ignore the others for now and you will notice almost immediate improvement. Here are some common problems and do-able solutions.

Terrible Spellers

The writing difficulty most commonly observed by teachers is spelling. Your students who are exceptionally poor spellers will seldom write willingly or well. In the third chapter, we discussed having a word wall of high-frequency words, modeling using that word wall while writing and requiring that students spell correctly the words on the wall in their writing. That will help most of your students but not students who misspell most of what they write. Children who do not spell well often spell all the words phonetically—assigning a letter to each sound. You can usually read most of what they write. Can you read these sentences?

> I cud not wat for my berthda to cum. I wil hav a parte. All my
> frends wil cum.

Did you understand that this child is eagerly anticipating her birthday and her party? Many children write text with every other word spelled incorrectly. Some older writers have been doing this for years and it is their habit. (This may happen if children are encouraged to spell words phonetically for several years without also receiving instruction in how to spell high-frequency words and common English spelling patterns. Encouraging children to use invented spelling is only a successful writing strategy if children are simultaneously given spelling instruction and expected to apply what they are learning as they write.)

Spelling is obviously this student's greatest need. How can you help solve this problem? In years past, there would not be a simple solution to this problem but there is today. Any good word-processing program with a spelling check will pick up most of the misspelled words and correct them. Children who have spelling as their greatest difficulty should type their first drafts on the computer and then run the spell check.

The spell-checking program will help make the piece more readable, and if you combine this with the use of a personal word wall, this student will—over time—become a better speller. To make a personal word wall, take a file folder and create a grid on the inside with room for words. Leave more space for letters like *s* and *t* than you do for *x*, *y*, and *z*. Each time this child writes and runs the spell

A animals	B because baseball birthday	C cousin catcher	D don't	E	F favorite friend
G gym great	H house	I	J	K kick	L laugh
M money	N night	O over	P party people	Q	R really
S sports school sister	T talk trucks they	U uncle	V vacation very	W want wasn't	X Y Z zoo

checker, let the child select one or two words to add to her personal word wall. Have the child tell you the chosen words and write them on that child's word wall with a permanent marker. No matter how many words are misspelled, do not let the child add more than two. When the child goes to the computer to write, she should open the file folder and review the words already there. This will take some time because the spelling of some high-frequency words such as *what* (WUT), *was* (WUZ), and *have* (HAV) is probably automatic but the child should be trying not to have any of these words show up when it is time to spell check. Each time the child writes, the text written that day is spell checked and one or two words are added to the personal word wall. Across many writing days, the child's spelling will improve. The child will delight in spelling *have* correctly and not letting the computer catch her on that one.

In addition, the first draft this child chooses to publish will have fewer spelling errors. This will make the revising, editing, and publishing steps much less frustrating for both you and the child and the child's attitude toward writing will show gradual improvement.

Is it fair to let this child write at the computer while the others write with pencils and paper? Yes, it is, because "fair" means giving every child what he or she needs most, not giving every child the same thing. If you have lots of children who want to do their first drafts on the computer, you might let children who choose to rotate days on which they get to write on the computer. If your class goes to the computer lab once or twice a week, having some students write their first drafts would be more worthwhile than some of the game/worksheet activities found on computers in many computer labs.

Almost all adults now do their first-draft writing on computers. Producing some first drafts on the computer will help all your students become more able and willing writers. For students for whom spelling is their major writing problem, writing on a computer with a spell check will greatly alleviate that problem.

Children with Unreadable Handwriting

In some cases, children's handwriting is so awful that you cannot read what they wrote. Some teachers suspect that some children use this poor handwriting so that no one can read what they wrote! Regardless of their motivation, children with terrible handwriting don't usually like to write and they are almost always embarrassed to have anyone see their writing. Again, a basic computer with a word-processing program is probably your best solution. Writing on the computer will not generally improve handwriting but most writing in college and in the workplace is now done on computers. Children with illegible handwriting will be better writers if allowed to do first drafts on the computer. There is no need to develop a personal word wall—unless you discover that the handwriting was hiding terrible spelling. Then, you can use the procedures just described to help your students become better spellers while removing the handwriting hindrance to writing.

Children Whose Writing Lacks Any Sense of Mechanics and Conventions

Some children write with very little or no punctuation or capitalization. The writing of these students is usually readable but hard to read and the editing task seems enormous. Here is an example. Have you seen this kind of writing before?

> my frend and i we was walking down the stret when we seen a big black dog with a broke leg he was in pain and looked pityful we ran to the vets and told him what we saw

Clearly, the biggest problem this writer faces is the lack of any sense of sentence or punctuation. (There are a few spelling errors, but sentence sense and punctuation are more obvious problems. Once the child develops some sentence sense, the computer spell check/personal word wall might be the next problem you tackle.) This child needs a personal editor's checklist that begins with the most basic rules. For children like this, you need to emphasize the positive and the items on your checklist need to be stated affirmatively and added when the child can accomplish these.

As often as you can, preferably at the end of each day's writing, do a quick "thumbs-up" edit activity in which you read each sentence with the child and give him or her a "thumbs up" for each sentence that makes sense. Remember, at this time, you are only reading for sense—ignoring all nonstandard English and the lack of punctuation (as hard as that is!). This piece contains three sentences all of which make sense.

> my frend and i we was walking down the stret when we seen a big black dog with a broke leg
>
> he was in pain and looked pityful
>
> we ran to the vets and told him what we saw

Read these sentences with your student, stopping at the end of each sentence and giving him a "thumbs up" for each sentence that makes sense. If, on another day, he has a sentence that doesn't make sense, give him a thumbs down and help him fix it. When you think the child is able to read his piece one sentence at a time and check for sense, let him read the sentences and be his own "thumbs up/down" editor and brag on the progress he is making. When the child accomplishes this most basic goal, begin his personal editor's checklist with a statement such as:

1. I can read my sentences for making sense.

This checklist can be a page in the child's notebook or taped to his writing folder.

On the day after you begin his checklist with this "I can" statement, tell him you want him to read his sentences one at a time for making sense and then check to see if there is ending punctuation at the end of the sentence. (As you were reading the sentences together for making sense, the child may have added ending punctuation without your prompting. Many children don't put ending punctuation because they have no sentence sense and don't know where one sentence ends and the next one begins. One confused writer finished his writing each day by going down the page and systematically putting a period at the end of each line! Once in a while, he lucked out and the end of the line coincided with the end of a sentence.)

A child who is writing like this probably won't need many question marks or exclamation points but as you are reading each sentence with him, point out any questions or exciting statements and praise him for varying his sentences! When the child can read most sentences and determine whether they make sense and include appropriate ending punctuation, add item 2 to the checklist.

2. I can check for ending punc. (. ? !)

Continue to add items to the checklist. Beginning capitals and capitals for I are obvious next items that will improve this child's writing. Once the child develops some sentence sense, the writing will look better and he will write more willingly. You can then decide to tackle the spelling or conventional English usage issues.

Children Whose Writing Shows Little Sense of Standard English

Teaching children whose spoken English is different from standard written English is a difficult but achievable task. Some computer programs have grammar checkers that will pick up common problems such as lack of subject/verb agreement, double negatives, and incorrect or unnecessary pronouns.

You might also want to start a chart such as the one we show here and add to it as you notice usage issues in the writing of the child. Again, you need to add items gradually to the chart and not expect change to occur overnight. Most of us wrote the way we spoke when we were in elementary school. Some of us were lucky enough to have parents whose spoken English was closer to standard written English. Teachers need to be careful not to tell children their speech patterns are "wrong" when these are the speech parents the significant adults in their lives use. It is much better to make a distinction between the way we talk and the way we write.

We Might Say . . .	But We Write . . .
We was walking.	We were walking.
We seen a dog.	We saw a dog.
He ain't home.	He isn't home.
He don't have no money.	He doesn't have any money.

Children with Little Prior Knowledge and Limited Vocabularies

It is hard enough to write when the writer knows a lot about the topic. Imagine how difficult (and discouraging) it is to write when someone is assigned a topic about which he or she knows very little. In Chapter 1, we encouraged you to begin your writing instruction at every grade level with single-draft writing in which your students selected their topics and wrote what they wanted to tell. In your early-in-the-year mini-lessons, you write about things you know many of your students also know about. You also model keeping a personal list of topics you might write about and encourage your students to create and add to a personal writing topics list. You may want to construct a class list of topics all your students know about. When your students are writing about topics they choose, they are writing about what they know. The prior knowledge/vocabulary problem is thus finessed!

But what can you do when you want all your students to write about a particular topic or learn to write a particular form? How do you keep lack of prior knowledge and vocabulary from being a huge roadblock for students whose knowledge of the world beyond their small neighborhood is very limited? Our solution is to anchor the topics you want all your students to write about in the various subjects you are teaching them. In Chapter 4, we described how using a variety of think-writes can help your students think more deeply about what they are learning. In Chapter 6, we proposed that students practice their editing skills as they write short pieces connected to their learning in science, math, social studies, and literature. In Chapter 8, we suggested that students learn to revise as they produce learning products that both demonstrate and increase their knowledge of various topics across the curriculum. You can alleviate the prior knowledge/vocabulary problem and increase content learning for all your students if you let the units you are teaching suggest the topics for most of the focused writing you have your students do. When you have them write across the curriculum, your students will write more, think more, learn more, and have more confidence in themselves as writers.

Children with No Knowledge of Different Writing Forms

As you observe the writing of your students during the first several weeks of school, you may notice children whose writing is all "personal narrative" or "all about me" writing. Again, this is fine if the children are first-graders but older children should have some variety of ways to write about different topics.

The first thing you need to think about if you notice this problem is, What kind of writing are you doing in your mini-lesson each day? Are you doing only "all about me" writing? Early in the year, it is natural for your students to write about themselves and their families, pets, and likes and dislikes, but you need to branch into some other genres fairly soon or you will, unintentionally, give older children the idea that this is the only kind of writing you expect to see. Before you begin teaching genres, you can model the writing of some genres in your mini-lesson:

> I love poetry. Today I am going to write a poem about my garden.
>
> I need to write an article for the school newsletter about our science fair. I will write it for my mini-lesson and you can help me make it as clear and interesting as possible.
>
> I saw many of you at the football game last night. I am going to pretend to be a reporter and write a newspaper article about the game.
>
> My son has a pet gerbil. We were researching gerbils on the Internet last night. I am going to write a report telling you the most interesting facts we learned about gerbils.

If you are writing a variety of different kinds of writing across the curriculum as described in Chapters 6 and 8, all your students will learn to write in different ways. Before that, however, you can model writing in a variety of ways so that your children understand that you value many different kinds of writing. Be sure that when a student shares writing that is a different genre, you comment positively on that achievement.

I loved your poem. I am so glad to see we have another poetry lover in the class.

That sounded like it could be a newspaper article. Have you thought about being a reporter when you grow up?

I loved your story, which was really a science fiction story. I bet you like to watch science fiction on TV and movies.

First-Draft Only "Once and Done" Writers

If your students come to you thinking that their first draft is the only kind of writing they do, you need to change their minds about that. Even though you are not doing the writing process during the first few weeks or months of school, be sure children know that this is where you are heading. Here are some things you can do early in the year to prepare your students for the writing process:

- Show some published pieces you have saved from previous years (or borrowed from another teacher).

- Invite the children to bring in books or other published pieces they have done in previous school years. The number of children who have anything to bring will let you know how much writing process they have actually experienced!

- Bring in a guest author and or/editor. (Suggestions for finding a local one are given in Chapter Five.) Have the guests bring some first drafts and published copies and talk about the revising, editing, and publishing steps every published piece goes through.

- Have your students save all their first drafts they are working on early in the year and have them choose one of them for their first published piece.

- Begin your editor's checklist and explain to the children that they will soon be publishing pieces and they will need to learn to become editors for themselves and each other.

- Occasionally comment that one of the pieces shared would make a "wonderful book once we get into publishing!"

- Take a piece of your writing through the writing process before you begin having your children publish pieces. If you let them watch you write the first draft of the Fieldtrip piece for the newsletter, let them help you revise it (make it *even* better) and edit it. When they take the newsletter home, have them brag to the parents about what they did to help you make it more interesting, more clear, and nearly perfect.

If you let your students know early that revising, editing, and publishing are all part of writing in your classroom, most will get over their "once and done" attitudes before you expect them to begin publishing.

Children with Physical Limitations

Included in most classrooms today are children with a variety of physical limitations that make writing difficult or impossible. Children with limited vision often cannot write with paper and pencil; those with speech difficulties often find writing and sharing their writing arduous; and children with cerebral palsy and various other physical problems may not be able to write with pencil and paper or even with the normal computer keyboard. This is an area in which special computer devices and programs are an absolute necessity to allow these children to learn to write. It is even more critical that these children learn to write because many lack fluent speech, and being able to write gives them a way to express themselves and participate in classroom life. No teacher can be expected to know the specifics of all the devices available. What you do need to know is that if you have a child with a physical disability that makes writing in the normal way impossible, there are devices that will allow this child to write. Also, by federal law, the child is entitled to have access to these devices, regardless of the cost. There are several websites where you can get the latest information about computer assistive technology. The website of the National Center to Improve Practice (www2.edc.org/NCIP) has information about educational technology as well as video clips of children with disabilities using these technologies. Linda Burkhart's website (www.lburkhart .com/links.htm) has ideas for using the Internet in the classroom for children with disabilities. Special Education Training British Columbia (www.setbc.org) has lots of information about assistive technology, including some books that may be downloaded for children who can't physically manage books in the traditional format.

Computer Assistive Devices and Software

Here are some of the computer assistive devices and software available now. Perhaps more advanced devices and programs will be available by the time this book is published.

Co:Writer (Don Johnston). Co:Writer is a talking word-prediction program. Based on what the child has written and the first few letters of the next word, it predicts what the whole word will be. Children can click on the word and it becomes part of the text. It also contains Flexspell, which translates phonetic spelling.

Write:Outloud (Don Johnston). Write:Outloud is a talking word processor that gives immediate speech feedback as students type words, sentences, and paragraphs. Its spell-check capability includes a Homonym Checker, which recognizes homonyms and offers definitions so that children can choose the correct word. Text can be read back to children. This program is particularly helpful for children with visual impairments.

Draft:Builder (Don Johnston). This program helps children organize ideas through a variety of visual maps. Speech feedback is included.

Kidspiration (Inspiration). This software is based on Inspiration but easier to use. It integrates pictures and writing to help children develop visual maps to connect and expand ideas. These maps, along with audio support, help children write organized text.

Special keyboards and other devices. For children who can't use a regular keyboard, there are special keyboards, switches, and eye-gaze pointers that allow children with limited mobility to word process and create text.

Children Whose Writing Lags Way Behind the Rest of the Class

In almost every class once we begin publishing, we have a few children whose writing is really not "edit-able." (Like love, this is hard to describe but you will recognize it when you see it!) We generally don't begin publishing until almost all of the children are writing something "readable," but this seems always to leave a few children whose pieces are collections of letters with a few recognizable words and very few spaces to help you decipher the letters from the words! You might say these children just aren't ready to publish and that they should just continue producing first drafts—but the message that most children would get from being left out of the publishing process is that, just as they thought, they can't write! Once you begin publishing, you need to include everyone in the process. Some children will have more published pieces than others. Some authors are more prolific than others. The goal is not for everyone to have the same number—and in fact we don't count and try not to let our students count. The goal is, however, for everyone to feel like a real writer because everyone has some published pieces.

Once you begin publishing, it is usually best to work with the most avid writers first, but when most of them have a piece published and are on their second round of first drafts, it's time to gather the children who have not yet published anything. Help them choose a piece they want to publish and then give them the option of reading or telling what they want to say. Encourage others in the group to make suggestions for revision as you make notes of what each child wants to write and the revision suggestions.

Then, sit down individually with each student and help the child construct his or her piece. Ask again for the child to tell you what he or she wants to say. As they tell, write their sentences by hand or type them on the computer. Once the sentences are written, we read them with the students several times to make sure they know what they have said. Then cut the sentences apart and have the children illustrate each sentence and put them all together into their book! They are now—like everyone else—real published authors and they approach their second round of first-draft writing with renewed vigor—confident that they too can write!

Notice that here you are willing to do something for your most struggling writers that you wouldn't ordinarily do for them because you don't want them to feel they can't keep up with the rest of the class and you want them to have published pieces that are readable by the other children. This dictation, however, takes place during the publishing time—and is not the way any of your students produce first drafts. If you were to let your most struggling writers dictate their first drafts to you or an assistant, you would be sending a clear message of, "You can't write and I don't expect you to learn to write."

English Language Learners

Anyone who has ever tried to learn a new language knows that the most difficult task in that new language is to write. When reading in a new language, people only have to recognize the words and language structures and think what they mean. When writing, people have to produce the words and the syntactic patterns in which they go together. Writing is a way to learn a language. Because writing is external, it is a way for you to see what misunderstandings your students have and to give them helpful feedback.

Children who are learning English will learn it faster if they are encouraged to write in English. That writing, however, must be supported, and any notion you might harbor that the writing should approach perfection must be put aside. Writing is hard enough when writing in one's first language; it is extra difficult when the syntax and vocabulary are unfamiliar. When helping English language learners write, put on your "coach" and "cheerleader" hats, celebrate small victories, and turn a blind eye to all the things that need fixing. This is not easy for most teachers to do, but if you can, you will be rewarded by watching your English language learners learn to write and make more rapid progress in their mastery of English. If you want your English language learners to become English speakers and writers as quickly as possible, put your red pen away and put your smiling face on and see writing as one more way for them to learn English.

English language learners need to participate in self-selected, single-draft writing as outlined in Chapters 1 and 2, just as everyone else does. They need to share their writing and receive both praise and questions about what they write. When you begin editing, revising, and publishing, they may need more help from you than students whose first language is English. You may want to use the suggestions listed in the previous section to help them produce published pieces they can be proud of.

The two most difficult areas of writing for English language learners are syntax and vocabulary. The remainder of this chapter will suggest practical strategies for supporting writers in these two areas.

Sentence Frames

Syntax is the way words go together to make sentences. Different languages have different syntaxes. In Spanish, for example, adjectives follow nouns and verbs are placed later in sentences. The Spanish equivalent of *I have a big dog* might be *Yo tengo un perro grande* (I have a dog big).

To write in English, children need to become familiar with English sentence order and other syntactic conventions. They also need to develop English vocabulary. Using a variety of frames and models can help them learn this. The simplest frames are sentence frames. We will give you some examples here and you will be able to come up with many frames that fit your students and your curriculum. When working with any of these frames, you will want to follow four steps:

1. Provide an experience.

2. Talk about it and create a list of words.

3. Model writing and then drawing.

4. Have your students write and then draw.

Here is a very simple example for early in the year with a class of children (of any age) who are just beginning to learn English.

Step 1: The Experience. The teacher brings in a variety of vegetables. The teacher and the children sample the vegetables and talk about them. They use the English name for each vegetable, and children may share the name for that vegetable in their first language.

Step 2: Talk and List. The teacher and the children talk about the vegetables and create a simple web with the different vegetable names and simple pictures.

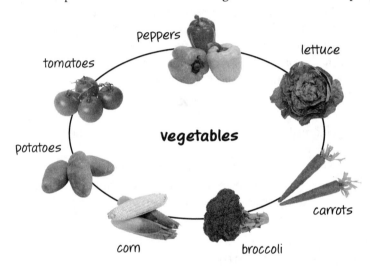

Step 3: Model Writing and Drawing. The teacher models drawing and writing a simple sentence about one of the vegetables.

I like carrots.

After the sentence is written, the teacher and the students read it chorally. The teacher draws a simple picture of a carrot.

Step 4: Have the Children Write and Draw. The children are given drawing paper. They copy the sentence frame:

I like

Next, they finish their sentence with their favorite vegetable, copying it from the web. They illustrate their writing and put their names on it.

Some of you may consider this writing lesson too simple, and it may be too simple for your English language learners, but it is the appropriate level for many children who are just learning English to be successful and develop positive, confident attitudes toward writing. Many teachers bind the pages each child creates into class books. Children love reading and rereading about themselves and their friends.

The basic steps of this lesson can be repeated again and again with a variety of experiences and with sentences that become more complex as the lessons go on. Here are some possibilities:

1. *Experience.* fruits
2. *Talk and List.* fruits
3. *Model Writing and Drawing.* I like apples and bananas.
4. *Have the Children Write and Draw.* I like _____ and _____ .
   (simpler: I like_____ . More complex: I like to eat _____ and _____ .)

1. *Experience.* actions (hop, run, jump, etc.)
2. *Talk and List.* actions
3. *Model Writing and Drawing.* I can hop and run.
4. *Have the Children Write and Draw.* I can _____ and _____ .
   (simpler: I can_____ . More complex: I can _____ , _____ ,
   and _____ .)

1. *Experience.* sports
2. *Talk and List.* sports
3. *Model Writing and Drawing.* I like to play soccer.
4. *Have the Children Write and Draw.* I like to play _____ .
   (More complex: My favorite sport is_____ .)

1. *Experience.* photos of people in family brought from home
2. *Talk and List.* brother, sister, mom, grandfather, and so on
3. *Model Writing and Drawing.* This is my grandma.
4. *Have the Children Write and Draw.* This is my _____ .
   (More complex: This is my _____ and my _____ .)

Sentence Combining Frames

After the children have gained control of some basic English syntax, you may want to give them some instruction in sentence combining to help them learn to write more complex syntax. Again, you want to start with an experience, have the children talk about the experience, and then create some kind of graphic organizer with the words. You can then model writing two simple sentences and combining them into one. Here is an example for the topic "Zoo Animals":

1. *Experience.* The class has been learning about zoo animals. They have watched many videos and taken virtual fieldtrips to zoos. They have read simple books about zoo animals and the teacher has read aloud a variety of books.

2. *Talk and List.* The teacher begins a chart to help the students summarize what they have learned about zoo animals. Different children contribute ideas to the chart. Here is what the beginning of the chart looks like:

Animal	Live	Eat	Look like	Move
Zebra	Africa Asia Zoos	Grass Leaves	Black and white Stripes Small horses	Run Gallop Jump
Monkey	Africa Asia Mexico South America Zoos	Fruits Vegetables Leaves Insects	Hands Feet Different sizes Different colors Fur	Climb Swing Jump Run
Elephant	Africa Asia Zoos Circuses	Grass	Long trunks Floppy ears Huge Wrinkly skin	Walk Run Swim
Tiger	Asia Zoos Circuses	Pigs Deer Baby animals	Orange fur Black and white stripes Sharp claws Big cats	Run very fast Stalk prey
Kangaroo	Australia Zoos	Greens Vegetables Fruits	Pouch Big back feet Pointy ears	Run Hop Kick
Bear				
Lion				
Giraffe				

3. *Model Writing.* The teacher chooses a mammal and writes two short sentences about that mammal.

> Tigers are big cats. They live in Asia and in zoos.

Next, the teacher models how these two sentences can be combined into one longer one.

> Tigers are big cats that live in Asia and in zoos.

The teacher may want to write two more simple sentences and show how these can be combined.

> Tigers are orange. They have black and white stripes.

> Tigers are orange with black and white stripes.

4. *Have the Children Write.* The children choose a zoo animal and write two short sentences about it. They share these sentences in small groups and decide how the sentences can be combined into one longer sentence.

Paragraph Frames

Paragraph frames can be used to help children learn the syntax of paragraphs. They follow the same four steps. Here is an example based on the same "Zoo Animals" topic. The Experience and the Talk and List steps are the same. The teacher chooses an animal and writes a simple paragraph about that animal, using the information from the chart.

> Elephants live in Asia and Africa. They eat leaves and grass. Elephants are huge animals with big floppy ears and long trunks. They eat leaves and grass. They can walk, run, and swim. Elephants are very big and interesting animals.

Next, the teacher replaces all the animal-specific words with blanks and, as the students watch, creates this paragraph frame. Students use this frame and the chart to write paragraphs about their chosen animal.

> _____ live in _____ and _____. They eat _____ and _____ . _____ are _____ animals with _____ and _____ . They eat _____ and _____ . They can _____ and _____ . _____ are _____ and _____ animals.

Looking Back
Writing Interventions

Writing may be the most difficult cognitive activity people do. Writers have to know a lot to write—a lot about the topic, a lot of vocabulary, a lot about how the language in writing works, a lot of words and how to spell them, a lot of rules and mechanics, and a lot of different forms and genres in which to write. Writers have to juggle all these different "balls" at the same time as they write. Writing is difficult—even for good writers who write a lot. Some children have particular writing problems. Once you identify the most pressing problem, provide that student with additional supports, such as:

- *Spelling:* Writers whose major problem is spelling can be greatly helped by producing their first drafts using a computer and a spelling checker and by referring to a portable word wall.

- *Handwriting:* Writers whose major problem is handwriting can be greatly helped by producing their first drafts using a computer.

- *Mechanics:* Writers who lack any sense of punctuation and capitalization need their own gradually developed editor's checklist.

- *Usage:* Writers who use mainly nonstandard English need common patterns displayed on a "We Might Say . . . But We Write . . . " chart.

- *Lacking Prior Knowledge and Vocabulary:* Have students write on self-selected topics or topics you are learning about in all the subjects you teach.

- *Writes Only Personal Narratives:* Vary what you write in your mini-lessons and write different forms across the curriculum.

- *"Once and Done":* Make clear from the beginning that students will soon be taking some of their first drafts through the writing process. Begin teaching simple editing and revising strategies as soon as students are writing willingly if not well.

- *Physical Limitations:* Seek out and use computer-assisted devices, special keyboards, and software that make writing and literacy possible for all children.

- *Uneditable Writing:* Let children dictate to you to publish, but require them to write first drafts just as everyone else does.

- *English Language Learners:* Provide experiences, build vocabulary, and model writing using simple sentence and paragraph frames.

Chapter 11

Research on Teaching Writing

Good writing ability is an essential skill for a good job in corporate America or state government:

> A survey of 120 major American corporations employing nearly 8 million people concludes that in today's workplace writing is a "threshold skill" for hiring and promotion among salaried (i.e., professional) employees. Survey results indicate that writing is a ticket to professional opportunity, while poorly written job applications are a figurative kiss of death. Estimates based on the survey returns reveal that employers spend billions annually correcting writing deficiencies. (National Commission on Writing, September 2004, p. 3)

> A survey of state human resources divisions by the National Governors Association concludes that writing is considered an even more important job requirement for the states' nearly 2.7 million employees than it is for the private-sector employees studied in the Commission's previous survey of leading U.S. businesses. Still, despite the high value that state employers put on writing skills, a significant numbers of their employees do not meet states' expectations. These deficiencies cost taxpayers nearly a quarter of a billion dollars annually. (National Commission on Writing, July 2005, p. 3)

By the time today's elementary students are ready to enter the job market, writing can also be expected to become an essential skill for many, if not most, support-level jobs in the private and public sectors.

If a larger percentage of today's elementary students are going to avail themselves of education beyond high school, it often requires some proficiency in academic writing. In fact, expository writing ability is and has long been an essential skill for success in many, if not most, college courses (Bridgeman & Carlson, 1984).

General Approaches to Improve Writing

Research has examined the four general approaches that have been taken by teachers, schools, and districts to improve student writing ability. Considerable research exists on the general approaches of grammar, process writing, writing strategy instruction, and comprehensive writing instruction.

Grammar

The teaching of grammar provides systematic and explicit instruction on parts of speech, parts of sentences, and types of sentences. The most consistent finding in writing research is that teaching grammar does not improve student writing (Hillocks & Smith, 2003; Graham & Perin, 2007a). In fact, of all the different kinds of writing instruction that have been investigated, grammar is far and away the least effective (Graham & Perin, 2007a). Students can be taught to write more mature sentences, but from sentence combining instruction (Graham & Perin, 2007a) rather than from grammar instruction. Traditionally, grammar has been taught under the assumption that it would improve student writing. The research is overwhelmingly clear that it does not accomplish that goal.

So What?

There is no traditional grammar instruction described or advocated in this book. Children are taught to write correctly, but not by being taught parts of speech, parts of sentences, or types of sentences. Children are taught mechanics and usage rules they can use when they write, not rules they can use in a language book exercise or on a worksheet. By eliminating time spent teaching grammar, you increase the time you have available for instruction that can help your students learn to write better.

Process Writing

The general approach usually called process writing has been found to be an effective way of teaching writing (Pritchard & Honeycutt, 2006), especially if the teachers receive professional development in the approach (Voss, 2001; Graham & Perin, 2007a). The process writing approach has consistently been found to be superior to a traditional presentational mode of teaching writing in which students are taught what good writing is and how to do it by teacher talk and examples of good writing, and then expected to apply what they were taught this way in a writing assignment (Hillocks, 1986).

Strategy Instruction for Writing

Students can be taught more sophisticated strategies for any phase of writing, whether these strategies are to be applied generally or in a particular kind of writing. Strategy instruction has the goal that students will eventually learn to use the strategies independently. Recent meta-analyses of research have found that strategy instruction has large effects and is the most valuable means of helping students become better writers (Graham, 2006; Graham & Perin, 2007a). Strategy instruction is particularly effective for struggling writers (Graham & Perin, 2007a). It is equally effective for younger and older students, and for learning how to produce different kinds of writing (Graham, 2006).

Some of the key components of writing strategy instruction are modeling the strategy, supporting students' use of the strategy in their own writing, and moving students to independent use of the strategy. Another essential element is criterion-based learning rather than time-based learning—that is, teaching or reteaching a strategy until students learn it, rather than for a set amount of time (Graham, 2006).

out sufficient repetition over time. There are teacher conferences, but often they are not focused enough. There are peer conferences, but often they are not guided enough. Students are expected to plan, write, revise, edit, and publish, but often without adequate preparation and instruction for many students to benefit much from the experience. If there is one thing that differentiates the process writing instruction in this book from that you may be familiar with, it is that we have attempted to integrate writing strategy instruction with process writing so both are more effective.

Planning Strategies. Students can be taught strategies to help them plan what they are going to write. For example, they can be taught to brainstorm ideas for the topic they have chosen or that has been assigned, to organize those ideas as they will be translated into the major parts of the paper, to translate that plan into a draft, and to modify the plan as needed while writing (Graham, 2006). Research has shown that better writing plans are associated with better writing (Chai, 2006).

So What?

We included the two-minute talk, graphic organizers, asking the Five W Questions about the writing, and other instruction in this book to help students learn planning strategies that work for them. Because modifying plans as needed while writing has been found to be an important planning strategy, we also cautioned against evaluating student papers based on whether they are consistent with what was planned. By these means, you can teach your students to plan better and that planning will often lead to improvements in their first drafts.

Revising and Editing Strategies. Students can also be taught strategies to use to revise and edit their papers. In general, teaching students revision and editing strategies has been found to have large effects on their writing (Graham, 2006).

When teaching students to revise or edit, it is not only important to have separate writing, revision, and editing steps but also to have students delay revising or editing a paper until sometime after they have written it. Chanquoy (2001) found that students in grades 3, 4, and 5 revised and edited more and better when revising and editing were delayed.

A very important part of revision and editing instruction entails teaching students to recognize and apply specific criteria to the evaluation of writing. Research has shown that this can substantially improve student writing from second grade to college (Hayes, 2004). Students benefit by being given specific criteria and taught to use them to evaluate their own papers so they will know where they need revision or editing (Hillocks, 1986; Graham & Perin, 2007a).

So What?

In this book, we explained how to teach a variety of specific revising and editing strategies and their applications in personal writing and writing across the curriculum. As the research supports, we tied these strategies to specific criteria that the students are taught to use to evaluate their own papers in order to guide their revision and editing. From first grade to middle school, children gradually are presented with new revision and editing strategies as they demonstrate proficiency applying previously taught strategies. When you teach your students an Editor's Checklist and other writing scales, you are teaching them how to read their own writing to determine what errors need to be corrected and what revisions would improve it. When you teach your students specific revision and editing strategies tied to the criteria on your Editor's Checklist and other writing scales, you are teaching them how to significantly improve their final drafts and eventually their first drafts. When you have your students write new first drafts regularly while you are teaching them how to revise, they can always have at least three new first drafts to choose from each time they select one they want to work on to make it better. By doing so, you not only overcome some of their resistance to revision but you also build in the delay between first-draft writing and revision and editing that research supports.

Comprehensive Writing Instruction

Coker's (2006) recent study with low-income children in urban elementary schools found that these students benefitted from a comprehensive writing program beginning in first grade. "Comprehensive" programs recognized the complexity of writing and the need for children to learn to integrate the various components of writing together. The most effective instruction was "developmental" in that it started where children were and moved them toward more sophisticated levels.

Other research has shown the importance of writing fluency in the overall mix of writing skills and strategies. From early on, rate of writing predicts later writing disability. Transcription skills (handwriting and spelling) uniquely predict writing fluency throughout the elementary grades (Graham, Berninger, Abbott, Abbott, & Whitaker, 1997). You build students' writing fluency when you teach them how to (1) spell words phonetically when they write, (2) spell high-frequency words correctly when they write, and (3) handwrite legibly when they write (Graham, Harris, & Fink, 2000).

So What?

In this book, we have described a large amount of instruction in process writing, writing strategies, and writing fluency in order to achieve a comprehensive writing program. Whether they are struggling, advanced, in-between, or some of all three, you can give your students comprehensive writing instruction that will help all of them learn to write significantly better than they did when they entered your classroom.

Specific Writing Instruction

In addition to supporting three of the four general approaches that teachers, schools, and districts take to improve students' writing ability, research has also been done on a variety of the specific teaching methods that comprise one or more of those three general approaches. The specific writing instruction that has been investigated includes modeling, prewriting activities, peers working together, self-selected writing, publishing, and student self-evaluation of writing.

Modeling

Research has contrasted the effectiveness of telling students how to write versus modeling for them. High levels of telling are negatively related to writing growth, whereas high levels of modeling are positively related, especially for children in high-poverty classrooms (Taylor, Pearson, Peterson, & Rodriguez, 2003). Modeling is one of the five instructional steps that collectively have been found to make writing strategy instruction most effective (Harris & Graham, 1996, 1999; Graham, 2006).

So What?

The research on modeling supports a central role for mini-lessons in an effective writing program. For example, to get your students off to a successful start in writing, you must show them that the thing you care most about in their writing is that they write what they want to tell and tell it in as interesting and genuine way as they can. You begin to do this by modeling in your own writing something you want to tell them—perhaps a memory from when you were their age. For another example, you show your children how and why you want them to invent spell by inventing spellings while you write during some of your mini-lessons. Remember that modeling is a valuable tool for you to use to teach any planning, writing, revising, or editing strategy you want your students to learn. It is far better than teacher talk at wiping that look of confusion off their faces!

Prewriting Activities

Prewriting activities in general have a small but consistently positive effect on the quality of student writing (Graham & Perin, 2007a; Sadoski, Willson, & Norton, 1997). Inquiry, in particular, has been found to be an effective kind of prewriting activity (Hillocks, 1986; Graham & Perin, 2007a; Sadoski, Willson, & Norton, 1997).

So What?

What you do before students begin writing a first draft is important and often takes time. You can improve your students' writing by carefully crafting good prewriting activities that prepare your students to be more successful when they write. Prewriting activities are particularly important for most writing across the curriculum.

Peers Working Together

Research has been conducted in grade 4 and higher on the effectiveness of collaborative arrangements in writing instruction. Having students work together to help each other with one or more facets of their writing has been found to have a strong positive impact on the quality of student writing (Graham & Perin, 2007a).

Likewise, Sadoski, Willson, and Norton (1997) found that peer conferencing improved writing in the elementary grades. "Students are also motivated by cooperative writing tasks that help them learn different strategies and styles from each other" (McCutchen, 1988).

According to other research, having peers work together improves revision and editing (Allal & Chanquoy, 2004). Zammuner (1995) found that the most changes were made to first drafts when children wrote individually but revised and edited in pairs. Holliway and McCutchen (2004) also found that peer response and editing helped student writers adopt the perspective of readers of their writing.

So What?

In this book, we have recommended and described how to have peers work together regularly, especially when they are learning revision or editing strategies. When you have your students work together in structured ways, you will improve both their writing abilities and their motivation.

Self-Selected Writing

Generally, students write more on topics they select than on topics they are assigned (Meichenbaum & Biemiller, 1992; Scardamalia & Bereiter, 1986). This seems to occur, in part, because children have significantly more content knowledge about topics they want to write about than they have about assigned topics (Gradwohl & Schumacher, 1989). "Children also sustain engagement longer in open-ended writing tasks than closed tasks and are more persistent when they experience difficulties" (Turner, 1993).

So What?

We have emphasized self-selected writing in the early grades and at the beginning of the year at every grade. In fact, establishing self-selected writing is so important, we hope you are willing for some of your students to write nothing for a few days in order for them to reap the benefits of self-selected writing when they do begin. Fortunately, we have found that teaching methods like The Five Steps or Can't Stop Writing, depending on the grade you teach, can help almost all your students do self-selected writing from the first day.

Publishing

Not much research has been done on publishing as a separate step of the writing process. Alber (1999) did find that publishing writing to be read by a known audience increases student motivation in first-draft writing, revision, and editing.

So What?

Because publishing can take over a writing program, working the teacher a lot harder than it works the students, we have downplayed traditional classroom book publishing in this book. We have suggested alternatives to individual children publishing more than one or two books across the year, and we have strongly recommended the KISS principle for publishing—Keep It Super Simple! Publishing can play a worthwhile support role in your writing program, but the most valuable thing it can do is to motivate your students to write, revise, and edit. Publishing of any kind that accomplishes that research-based goal is sufficient; so, don't get carried away!

Student Self-Evaluation of Writing

Sadoski, Willson, and Norton (1997) found that elementary school writing was improved when teachers used specific criteria in both instruction and assessment. "Assigning students product goals for their writing has a strong impact on its quality" (Graham & Perin, 2007a). Going the additional step of teaching students to use these criteria to evaluate their papers, including their own, has been shown to substantially improve student writing across a wide range of writing ability (Hayes, 2004).

So What?

In this book, we provided examples of teaching students specific criteria for every aspect of their writing. We also described how you can teach these criteria using mini-lessons and other means and then add them to writing scales, such as an editor's checklist, or an information checklist, for your students to use to self-evaluate their writing in order to guide their revision and editing. Teaching your students to be able to evaluate their own writing to know what it needs is the single-most important thing you can do to help them become independent writers. Their future teachers and employers may not thank you, but they should!

Connecting Reading and Writing

Two ways of connecting reading and writing have been investigated by writing researchers. The first of these, the study of good examples of writing, is a part of traditional presentational writing instruction, particularly at the secondary level (Hillocks, 1986). The second, summarization, is often associated with writing across the curriculum.

The Study of Good Examples of Writing

Researchers have found a small but consistently positive effect on the quality of student writing of the study of well-written examples by children's authors of the kind of writing students are trying to learn to do. However, these researchers have also pointed out that there are a number of more effective instructional strategies for improving student writing (Hillocks, 1986; Graham & Perin, 2007a).

So What?

Because it has been found to have a small effect, we have focused very little on the study of good examples of writing in this book. We do use examples from children's favorite books occasionally in our lessons, but when we do so, we usually make the example more powerful and focused by first presenting a version we have rewritten so it lacks whatever particular features the example has that we want the students to attend to.

Summarization

Studies have taught students in grade 5 and higher to summarize texts they read. The findings of these studies support the practice, indicating that summarization instruction has a strong effect on improving the conciseness of student writing (Graham & Perin, 2007a).

> ## So What?
>
> In this book, we use summarization in writing across the curriculum to enhance students' content learning while improving the conciseness of their writing. You can have your students do "What I learned"/summary quick-writes, turn the **L** column into a summary at the end of a KWL lesson, as well as produce and revise summaries as one kind of written learning product. When you teach your students to summarize, you achieve a balance between content learning and writing instruction.

Writing to Learn

Having students write during science, social studies, literature, and other subject-matter instruction generally increases their learning of those subjects (Bangert-Drowns, Hurley, & Wilkinson, 2004; Graham & Perin, 2007b). Writing across the curriculum results in small but consistently positive effects on student performance on teacher tests, report card grades, and standardized test scores, compared with conventional content instruction that does not include writing to learn (Bangert-Drowns, Hurley, & Wilkinson, 2004). Even brief writing-to-learn tasks can enhance learning, but having students write to learn regularly over time yields greater gains in content knowledge (Bangert-Drowns, Hurley, & Wilkinson, 2004). Writing to learn improves achievement across the curriculum even more when students are prompted to include reflections about their current state of knowledge, any confusion they may have, or how they are trying to learn the subject (Bangert-Drowns, Hurley, & Wilkinson, 2004).

> ## So What?
>
> This book includes writing across the curriculum as an integral part of the writing instructional program at every elementary grade. We have delineated writing across the curriculum to enhance students' content learning while teaching them how to write better—not primarily to assess what students know or have learned. You can use a variety of think-writes to help your students learn more in every area of the curriculum by getting them to activate prior knowledge, make predictions, or construct brief summaries. You can add repetition with variety to content learning, motivate student interest and discussion in both writing and content, and provide

additional practice in learning to edit their own writing by having your students write poems of various kinds, postcards, letters, interviews, and other short pieces for each other to read. You can improve both learning and writing ability by having your students write learning products that demonstrate their current knowledge or attitudes about various areas of the curriculum. Then, you can increase their learning and writing ability even more by having them revise some of their learning products by adding academic vocabulary or examples, using an information checklist to ensure that all essential facts are included, and so on.

Writing Engagement and Motivation

In elementary classrooms, increased engagement of children with writing tasks can be accomplished by a combination of efforts on the part of the teacher. Large amounts of positive motivation, as well as making sure instruction does not undermine student motivation to write are both important (Bogner, Raphael, & Pressley, 2002; Pressley, 2002). To refine these efforts, research supports two major emphases: building students' intrinsic motivation to write and building their self-efficacy in writing.

Intrinsic Motivation in Writing

"Intrinsic motivation concerns the performance of activities for their own sake, in which pleasure is inherent in the activity itself" (Gottfried, Fleming, & Gottfried, 2001, p. 3). Extrinsic motivation is engaging in an activity in order to receive a reward. Anything you choose to do out of interest, enjoyment, curiosity, or desire for self-improvement is intrinsically motivated. Elementary students in third grade and higher who are intrinsically motivated tend to get better grades and score higher on standardized tests (Gottfried, Fleming, & Gottfried, 2001; Lepper, Corpus, & Iyengar, 2005). However, the earlier in school that teachers begin building students' intrinsic motivation, the more likely the approach is to work (Gottfried, Fleming, & Gottfried, 2001).

Reducing the use of extrinsic rewards has been shown to help build students' intrinsic motivation (Cameron & Pierce, 1994). A number of researchers have also found that students perform better and longer on academic tasks and enjoy their participation more when they are given choices (Cordova & Lepper, 1996). Choice helps students increase their intrinsic motivation (Gottfried, Fleming, & Gottfried, 2001; Oka, 2005) and self-efficacy (Walker, 2003).

So What?

To help your students begin to acquire intrinsic motivation in writing, nothing is more important than the attitude you regularly express toward your writing and theirs. Your enthusiasm about what you write about during mini-lessons can be contagious, and it will show your students that writing does not have to be a chore, but should be seen as an opportunity to tell someone something interesting, important, or fun. When you find things to respond positively to in your students' writing, you are supporting the development of their intrinsic motivation for writing.

By teaching children that they can write about what they already care about, you help them overcome the lack of intrinsic motivation they may have in writing about a topic they don't care about. When children refuse to write unless teachers give them a topic, they are basically saying that they consider writing to be something kids do in school but that it has no relationship to their real lives. You can use self-selected writing to gradually change your students' attitudes that writing is a school-based rather than a personal activity.

Prediction think-writes are another way of building or tapping into intrinsic motivation. When students make a prediction, they want to find out whether their prediction was right. That is intrinsic motivation—milk it for all it's worth!

Self-Efficacy in Writing

People used to think that motivation was all about feelings. Research in recent decades has shown that beliefs are also an essential component of motivation. In particular, self-efficacy has been shown to contribute to student engagement and success with academic tasks. "Self-efficacy refers to beliefs a person has about his or her capabilities to learn or perform behaviors" (Schunk & Zimmerman, 1997, p. 34). Studies have consistently found that students' self-efficacy in writing is related to how well they write (Pajares, 2003). If students believe they can learn to write better, for example, they are more likely to be willing to write, to try hard when they write, to persist when the going gets tough, and to avoid stress when writing under pressure. If students believe they may fail to learn to write better, they are more likely to try to avoid writing or, if they can't avoid it, to finish it quickly with as little effort as possible.

Research has found at least four mutually supportive ways you can build your students' self-efficacy in writing. The first way is to increase their writing successes and reduce their writing failures (Schunk & Zimmerman, 1997). Students who have usually been successful in their writing expect to be successful next time; students who have usually failed expect to fail next time (Walker, 2003). It will not always be possible for you to ensure success or prevent failure, but successful writing teachers consider what they do and say to their students in light of how it may affect their self-efficacy. As one aspect of reducing writing failures, research has found that lowering the competitive orientation of a classroom increases students' self-efficacy (Pajares & Valiante, 2006). It is also helpful when teachers give feedback to students about their writing in terms of the gains they are making (Bandura, 1997).

So What?

To help students increase their writing successes and reduce their writing failures, always express enthusiasm for some aspect of each student's writing. Teach writing strategies, but have a tolerance for imperfection! Have your students do single-draft writing until they are writing willingly, before teaching them to edit. Don't teach them to revise until they can edit. Keep the time they are required to write short at first and only gradually increase it. Teach and require them to invent spell and use the word wall so that they don't feel like a failure because of spelling. Teach them to respond positively to each other's writing, and consider any derogatory remark by one child of another's writing a disciplinary problem. Help your students compare their writing now with their writing in the past so they can see that they have improved.

The second proven way to build students' self-efficacy in writing is to teach them strategies they can use to perform better while writing (Schunk & Zimmerman, 1997). Learning specific writing strategies contributes to students' beliefs that they can learn how to write better, and it helps students have more success when they write, which contributes additionally to their self-efficacy in writing. In fact, raising students' skill levels in a way that gives them more genuine success experiences with a particular aspect or type of writing has recently been found to be the best way to build self-efficacy in writing (Pajares, Johnson, & Usher, 2007).

So What?

This book is filled with writing strategy instruction, not only because research says it is highly effective in improving writing but also because research says it builds self-efficacy in writing. For both reasons, it is vital to teach children the essential strategies of writing and not assume that they will learn how to write well just by writing.

The third way to boost your students' self-efficacy in writing is to use modeling. Research has found that modeling how to cope when having trouble is more effective than modeling mastery (Schunk & Zimmerman, 1997). That is, models that show difficulty and how to overcome it with effort, persistence, or a specific strategy build students' self-efficacy better than models that show performing the task without error.

So What?

As we have explained earlier in this chapter, good mini-lessons—with clear teaching points and sufficient repetition—are an important part of writing strategy instruction because they show, rather than tell, your students how to do some important aspect of writing. Also to build students' self-efficacy and teach them how to cope with difficulties, it is very important that your mini-lessons model you having and overcoming difficulties! Specifically, model invented spelling, making errors you correct during editing, writing a boring draft you revise so it is more interesting, adding essential information to your draft that lacked it, and so forth. To have self-efficacy, students must know how to overcome problems without thinking that having problems is an indication of failure. There is no better way to teach them that than to model it.

The fourth way to increase self-efficacy is to teach your students to monitor and evaluate their own performance in writing (Pajares & Valiante, 2006). Providing students with specific criteria they can use to evaluate their own writing helps to build their self-efficacy (Schunk, 2003). When students see specific opportunities to improve their papers by applying strategies you have taught them, their self-efficacy improves. "Negative self-evaluations will not diminish self-efficacy and motivation if students believe they are capable of succeeding but that their present approach is ineffective" (Schunk & Zimmerman, 1997, p. 40). Rather, finding errors or missing elements in one's own writing provide opportunities to set their own specific short-term goals that can be met and then contribute to self-efficacy (Schunk & Zimmerman, 1997).

Writing Assessment

An emphasis on preparing students for an upcoming writing test narrows writing instruction so that other goals of writing instruction are abandoned or severely downplayed (Hillocks, 2002; Pedulla, Abrams, Madaus, Russell, Ramos, & Miao, 2003; Barone, 2006). Teachers and administrators appear to believe that such an emphasis will lead to significantly better scores on their local or state high-stakes writing test. However, test preparation beyond a minimum amount soon reaches diminishing returns. Because it displaces instruction that would actually improve student writing, continued test preparation often results only in mediocre test score gains (Barone, 2006) and little or no improvement on long-term writing performance (Pedulla, Abrams, Madaus, Russell, Ramos, & Miao, 2003).

In most schools, it is necessary to grade students' writing and mark their papers in order to give them grades on their report cards and to be able to defend those grades, but research makes it clear that grading and marking their papers teaches them little or nothing:

> Teacher comment [written on students' compositions] has little impact on student writing. None of the studies of teacher comment . . . show statistically significant differences in the quality of writing between experimental and control groups. Indeed, several show no pre-to-post gains for *any* groups, regardless of the type of comment. (Hillocks, 1986, p. 165, emphasis in original)

So What?

Of course, teachers have to grade some of what students write. However, we have largely ignored grading in this book because it has no instructional value. Instead, we have filled this book with practices that do have instructional value. Grade your students as your school's grading system requires you to do, but do your best to keep the grades you give from undermining your students' intrinsic motivation and self-efficacy in writing.

Book Study Guide
for
What Really Matters
in Writing

Prepared by Sharon Arthur Moore
Consultant, L.E.A.D., Literacy Enrichment and Development

Book Study Guidelines

Reading, reacting, and interacting with others about a book is one of the ways many of us process new information. Book studies are a common feature in many school districts because they recognize the power of collaborative learning. The intent of a book study is to provide a supportive context for accessing new ideas and affirming best practices already in place. Marching through the questions in a lockstep fashion could result in the mechanical processing of information; it is more beneficial to select questions to focus on and give them the attention they deserve.

One possibility to structure your book discussion of *What Really Matters in Writing* is to use the Reading Reaction Sheet on page 218. Following this format, make a copy for each group member. Next, select a different facilitator for each chapter. The facilitator will act as the official note taker and be responsible for moving the discussion along. He or she begins by explaining that the first question is provided to start the group discussion. The remaining three questions are to be generated by the group. The facilitator can ask each person to identify at least one question and then let the group choose the three they want to cover, or the facilitator can put the participants into three groups, with each group responsible for identifying one question. The three questions are shared for all to hear and (and write down), and then discussion of Question 1 commences. The facilitator paces the discussion so the most relevant information for that group is brought out. Since many school districts require documentation for book studies, the facilitator could file the sheet with the appropriate person as well as distribute a copy to all group members for their notes.

Another possibility is to use the guiding questions for each chapter. You could have the same facilitator for all chapters. Perhaps this would be someone who read the book first and suggested it to the group. Or the facilitator role could rotate. It is suggested that the facilitator not only pace the group through the questions to hit on the most important information for the group's needs, but he or she should take notes for later distribution to group members and/or administrators if required for documentation.

The provided questions are meant to provoke discussion and might lead the group into areas not addressed in the questions. That is wonderful! The importance of a book study is to move the members along in their understanding of the book content. If time is limited, the facilitator might select certain questions from the list for the initial focus of the discussion, allowing other questions as time permits.

Of course, a third option is to combine the two structures. Select the format that best fits your group and the time frame you have set for completion of the book.

All book sessions should end with a purpose for reading the next chapter. It could be to generate questions the group still has, to find implications for each person's own teaching, or to identify new ideas. Purpose setting is a time-honored way to help readers (of any age) approach the text. If you are using the questions that accompany each chapter, direct the participants to read the questions prior to reading the chapter. This will provide a framework for processing the information in the chapter.

Book Study Questions for Each Chapter

chapter 1: Getting Writing Off to a Good Start

1. What strategies from this chapter do you see yourself using? Why?

2. Generate a question this chapter caused you to wonder about. Bring it to the group for discussion.

3. Think back to your school years. What are your memories of writing? How effective were the strategies you were taught? If one of those teachers were sitting here today, what would you say to that teacher?

4. In this chapter, the authors anticipate several of your frustrations with beginning a regular writing curriculum. Prior to reading their responses, discuss with your colleagues how you deal with:

   "Some of my students refuse to write. How do you get everyone to be willing to write?"

"If I let them choose what to write about, many of my students won't write."

"When I let them choose, they just write the same thing over and over."

"My class won't write if I don't spell for them!"

5. Now that you have read the proposals for dealing with the concerns from the chapter listed in Question 4, how do you see yourself implementing the suggestions? What else do you need to know to ensure a successful start to your writing program?

6. Having advanced writers can be a blessing in disguise for some teachers. Do you sometimes just feel grateful for having a few good writers in your classroom? Have you ever felt that you are not extending their writing? Do you wonder how to extend them? What would help you do that better?

7. Try out one or more of the suggestions for lessons in this chapter and come to the group for a discussion of your various experiences. Extend the ideas in this chapter with your own ways of "getting writing off to a good start."

8. While you were reading the description of upcoming chapters in the Preface, which sounded the most intriguing? Why? What do you expect to learn there?

chapter 2: What Do I Do Once I Have Them Writing?

1. What strategies from this chapter do you see yourself using? Why?

2. Generate a question this chapter caused you to wonder about. Bring it to the group for discussion.

3. Do you view yourself as a writer? Why or why not? Is it important to be a writer to teach children how to write? Why? What do you think the effect of being a writer (or not) might have on how you teach writing?

4. Even adult writers will ask published authors where they get their ideas. Apparently, choosing what to write about is perceived as one of the more difficult parts of the writing process. Do you agree? Why? Deconstruct the process of choosing and decide what underlies the difficulty of topic selection.

5. How often does your class write and for how long? Why? Do you start each day with a mini-lesson? How difficult is it to choose the focus for the mini-lesson?

6. How do you identify what your students' writing interests and needs are? How do you use that information when planning instruction?

7. Describe some of the strategies you have used to keep students writing. How successful were they? Why?

8. The "writ is it" syndrome is typical among students ("I wrote it already, so it's done"). Too often they see second-draft writing as merely copying over the first draft neatly. Helping them extend their writing and to see writing as a *process* as much as a *product* is one of your real challenges. Describe your experiences with helping students expand their writing into other drafts.

9. What are your favorite writing planning tools or devices? Why? Describe how you use them.

10. What are the ways you have your students share their writing? Why do you do it that way? What are your successes and challenges?

chapter 3: Spelling Matters!

1. Were you a "good speller" while in school? What were the factors that contributed to your spelling achievement?

2. Generate a question this chapter caused you to wonder about. Bring it to the group for discussion.

3. English is a very complex language. It's a wonder anyone ever learns to spell it! What are the specific elements you should be aware of as you try to help children predict spellings?

4. Is there a relationship between "word wonder" (a fascination with words) and spelling? Is there any beneficial effect on spelling from having a large meaning vocabulary? Discuss your experiences with students who can spell well (or not) and their meaning vocabularies.

5. What makes the word wall words (high-frequency words) harder to spell? What is an aspect of high-frequency words that helps with spelling?

6. There is a controversy in schools about how much to help students with spelling and how much latitude to allow them when using phonics spellings. This controversy is especially pertinent with public display of student writing (including sending home pieces with inaccurate spelling). Discuss your experiences with getting writing ready for "publishing."

7. Have you used any of the activities in this chapter? How successful were they? Which new activities do you plan to use? Why?

chapter 4: Think-Writes: Writing to Learn across the Curriculum

1. What strategies from this chapter do you see yourself using? Why?

2. Generate a question this chapter caused you to wonder about. Bring it to the group for discussion.

3. The concept of "think-writes" is probably a new way for you to think of everyday occurrences. Make a list (a think-write!) of the think-writes you have done today. Compare your think-writes with those written by others in your group. Discuss how you could share your personal experiences with think-writes to help your students see writing as a regular, ongoing, varied activity, one not limited to the traditional research paper.

4. Think of a lesson you are preparing to teach this week. In your plan book, include at least one think-write for that lesson. Bring it to your book study group to share with others and get ideas from them for their think-write inclusions.

5. In this chapter, think-writes are described as a way to "get more bang for your buck" in content-area learning. The focus here has been on the content areas. Discuss the differences and similarities when think-writes are used with a literary piece versus science or social studies content.

6. Several purposes for think-writes are described in the chapter. Discuss with your group how you could use them for activating prior knowledge, predicting, and summarizing. Which do you think your students will find easier to use initially? Why?

7. Students would likely enjoy having "thinking pens." What are some challenges with using them that you need to anticipate so the implementation goes smoothly day after day?

chapter 5: Editing Matters!

1. What strategies from this chapter do you see yourself using? Why?

2. Generate a question this chapter caused you to wonder about. Bring it to the group for discussion.

3. It is generally agreed in the writing field that it is easier to learn editing than revising. Do you agree with that perspective? Why?

4. One of the biggest battles with editing is convincing students of the need. What are some ways you convince students that "editing matters"?

5. One of the precautions in the chapter is to not begin editing until your students are writing with ease. What if the students come to you *not* writing easily but having spent the years before you doing required editing? How will you or how have you helped them make the transition to being comfortable writers who edit their work? Will you back up to the one-rule-for-the-day suggestion? Why?

6. Some teachers have their students skip lines for edits and revisions. Others give students scissors, tape, and extra paper to provide editing room. What have you done to ensure space for editing and how did that work for you? What are some concerns you should anticipate if you ask students to skip lines while writing and what will you do about that?

7. In one school system, teachers contacted their high school to find out what editing marks were required there. The teachers then backed those down from eighth grade to kindergarten so they could build an editing foundation for students to take with them from elementary and middle school. Obtain an editing marks copy from your local high school and build your own sequential set of editing marks for your school.

chapter 6: Writing and Editing across the Curriculum

1. What strategies from this chapter do you see yourself using? Why?

2. Generate a question this chapter caused you to wonder about. Bring it to the group for discussion.

3. What are the advantages of having students write short, edited pieces as a transition from think-writes to extended writing? What are the challenges?

4. A variety of poetry formats allow for students to produce short pieces. Which of these have you already used successfully? Unsuccessfully? Why? With what other poetry formats have you had success?

5. Poetry, postcards, notes, letters, interviews, and word problems are all types of writing that require the production of short pieces. Which of these have you used on an ongoing basis (not just in a letter-writing unit)? Why? How successful were they? What are some similar genres you have used regularly?

6. What were your writing goals for the genres listed in Question 5? How would making editing the focus goal change how you use these genres in your classroom? Discuss whether you can have more than one focus for a piece of writing.

7. One powerful advantage of regularly using the types of writing in this chapter is that many are real-life writing experiences, not just in-school writing. Discuss the long-term impact of making letter writing (or some other genre) a regular part of school writing.

chapter 7: Revision Matters!

1. What strategies from this chapter do you see yourself using? Why?

2. Generate a question this chapter caused you to wonder about. Bring it to the group for discussion.

3. Sometimes even teachers confuse editing and revising. Discuss some succinct differences with examples that you could share with a teacher (or parent) who confuses editing and revising.

4. One way to show students that published writers revise their work (and why should students think they are better than that!) is to bring copies of college textbooks to show what edition a text is. (Of course, you should bring one that is at least the second edition.) It is even better if you can have successive editions of the same text so you can show where authors made their changes. Seeing that people who make money from their writing understand the need for changes helps make your case for the need for their revisions.

5. Discuss the four strategies for revision described in this chapter. Had you ever considered the simplicity of explaining revising as ARRR (adding, replacing, reordering, or removing)? How would this help your students not only to revise but also to discuss revisions with you or other students?

6. Compare the ways members of your book study group teach revision with the order of the four strategies in this chapter. Why is this order of the strategies more powerful, or is it?

7. Think of your own writing. Do you struggle with revision? Why? How can you translate your own experiences with revision for students? If revision is easy for you and something you enjoy, how can you translate *that* experience for your students to learn from?

8. Revising as you write (just as happens with editing) is so subconscious with those who write a lot that they may not even be aware that they are revising and editing as they go. What does it take to get to that point? How can you help your students achieve that goal?

chapter 8: Revising across the Curriculum

1. What strategies from this chapter do you see yourself using? Why?

2. Generate a question this chapter caused you to wonder about. Bring it to the group for discussion.

3. Many years ago, a writing expert, Janet Emig, said that writing is a mode of learning, a way to deepen your understanding of your topic. Discuss with your group if you agree with Emig. Also, discuss whether or not, and in what ways, revising deepens understanding.

4. Writing for others to learn from (not as writing for the teacher to read and grade) can have an impact on revision. Discuss how having an authentic audience for writing whenever possible might affect students' understanding and acceptance of the need for revision.

5. What have been the biggest challenges you have faced with students as they revise their work in the content areas? What are some successful strategies you tried? Unsuccessful? Why did some things work and not others?

6. Discuss with your colleagues some examples of revisions you all have made. Compile this list so you can show your students what their teachers have been writing and revising (research paper for a graduate class, application for a science mini-grant, proposal to the school board for a policy change, letter to the editor about recycling, etc.). Having drafts of your efforts would show students that revision is a skill needed into adult life, not just in school.

7. Does your school use a writing scale to guide revisions? What are the challenges you face with the scale? What ways have you tried to introduce and maintain focus on the scale?

8. Have your students use their writing scale on one of their texts. Learning to evaluate another's writing gives insight into the elements of good writing. In Chapter 11 you will find there is little transfer to their own writing, but students will learn their writing scale more deeply by using it for analysis. Published writing used for analysis is called a "mentor text," meaning that the text is used to teach the concept demonstrated. Try this with your group to see what understandings of the writing scale you gain. Bring in a text the students use and use your writing scale to analyze it.

chapter 9: Sharing and Publishing

1. What strategies from this chapter do you see yourself using? Why?

2. Generate a question this chapter caused you to wonder about. Bring it to the group for discussion.

3. The term *publishing* can be misleading, since a published piece is just a shared piece of writing (made public) that has gone through some systematic revision and editing. Some teachers avoid publishing because of the extra work required on their part and the part of the student. When publishing takes longer than writing, there is a problem. Discuss how you make publishing work in your classroom.

4. Sometimes teachers come to their classroom writing program with some left-over negative feelings from their own student days. Talk about how your writing was made public and how you felt about publishing when you were a student.

5. What have you done to encourage reluctant writers to share their work? Why are they reluctant, and how did you address those concerns?

6. Teachers might feel less comfortable conferring with the two extremes of writers in their classrooms: the capable, fluent writer and the struggling writer. Sometimes it is hard to know what to say to extend a piece of writing when it is better than anyone else's in the class, or when it has so many problems you don't know where to begin. How do you handle these conferences? What would help you be a better teacher for these students?

7. Have you had success teaching your students how to interact with others in conferences? Do your students ask meaningful questions that will help extend the other students' writing? Describe your experiences with using peers to give feedback on writing.

8. Bring some of your students' published writing to the group. Share how you did it, how long it took, and what you felt your greatest successes and struggles were with producing the published works.

chapter 10: Writing Interventions

1. What strategies from this chapter do you see yourself using? Why?

2. Generate a question this chapter caused you to wonder about. Bring it to the group for discussion.

3. Throughout this book, the chapters have included "what if" and "what about" scenarios. Many of these require an alternative approach, a kind of writing intervention. What are some "what ifs" and "what abouts" you did not see addressed? Bring them to your group for discussion.

4. This chapter addressed the categories of terrible spellers, unreadable handwriting, lack of conventions and mechanics, limited oral English proficiency, limited meaning vocabulary, limited genre knowledge, "writ is it" writers, physical limitations, "way behind" writers, and English language learners. Are there any other categories of struggling writers the authors could have addressed? What percentage of your students fit each of these categories? What strategies have worked best for you with these students?

5. Some teachers and parents have trouble with the idea of using a computer to locate students' spelling errors or to overcome handwriting issues. Discuss why this is the case with your group. Talk about this strategy and others that would help struggling spellers and those with poor handwriting. How do you personally feel? Why?

6. Nonstandard English may be used by both monolingual English students as well as English language learners. Are there common strategies to help each group? What are the specialized (for each group) strategies you have used to help students demonstrate standard English in writing even if not in oral language? What do you struggle with while teaching these students to write standard English?

7. Most people demonstrate a larger vocabulary range in writing than in speaking. Why is that? How do you help your students acquire a more robust vocabulary that they can use while writing? What three strategies have you found most effective for building a rich writing vocabulary?

8. How have you gotten your struggling writers to move beyond first-draft writing? What was most successful and what didn't work well at all? Why?

chapter 11: Research on Teaching Writing

1. What strategies from this chapter do you see yourself using? Why?

2. Generate a question this chapter caused you to wonder about. Bring it to the group for discussion.

3. This chapter provided you with the rationale and research support to provide the kind of writing instruction students need and deserve. There is so much pressure on teachers to improve student test scores that sometimes teachers feel they are unable to do what is right, and instead just do what is required. Discuss with your group to what degree your writing instructional practices are reflective of test score pressures.

4. Did the authors omit any substantive issue you deal with? What is the issue? What information do you need to support your instruction in that area?

5. The authors present the four general approaches traditionally used as frameworks for classroom writing instruction (grammar-based, process writing, strategy instruction, and comprehensive writing instruction). Which one or ones do you focus on? Why? Describe your successes and struggles implementing your framework.

6. The authors also describe six specific writing instructional methods with research support: modeling, prewriting, peers working together, self-selected writing, publishing, and student evaluation of writing. Which ones of these do you systematically incorporate into your classroom writing program? Why?

7. What are your successes and struggles with implementing the six writing methods in Question 6? What have you learned about each of them and what else do you need to know to use them more effectively?

8. Many years ago, Dr. David Pearson said that comprehension and composition are two sides of the same coin. What do you think he meant by that? How can you take that concept into your classroom instruction?

9. What is the effect of writing across the curriculum in your classroom? How could you deepen the effect?

10. Sometimes students just aren't "into" writing. Maybe you aren't either. What have you done to increase attitude, interest, and motivation for writing in your classroom. Why? Discuss your successes and struggles with student engagement in the writing process.

11. Grading writing is one of the hardest tasks for teachers. What makes grading writing so hard? What has supported you in learning to better evaluate student writing?

Reading Reaction Sheet

Facilitator/Recorder (person who initiated the discussion): _____

Group reactants: _____

_____

Date of reaction/discussion: _____

Chapter title and author(s): _____

_____

Question #1: What ideas and information from this chapter could be used in classroom instruction?

Reactions:

Question #2: _____

_____

Reactions:

Question #3: _____

_____

Reactions:

Question #4: _____

_____

Reactions:

References

Alber, S. (1999). "I don't like to write, but I love to get published": Using a classroom newspaper to motivate reluctant writers. *Reading & Writing Quarterly, 15,* 355–361.

Allal, L., & Chanquoy, L. (2004). Introduction: Revision revisited. In L. Allal, L. Chanquoy, & P. Largy (Eds.), *Revision: Cognitive and instructional processes* (pp. 1–7). Boston: Kluwer.

Bandura, A. (1997). *Self-efficacy: The exercise of control.* New York: W. H. Freeman.

Bangert-Drowns, R. L., Hurley, M. M., & Wilkinson, B. (2004). The effects of school-based writing-to-learn interventions on academic achievement: A meta-analysis. *Review of Educational Research, 74,* 29–58.

Barone, D. (2006). High-stakes assessment and writing instruction. *National Reading Conference Yearbook, 55,* 99–109.

Bogner, K., Raphael, L., & Pressley, M. (2002). How grade 1 teachers motivate literate activity by their students. *Scientific Studies of Reading, 6,* 135–165.

Bridgeman, B., & Carlson, S. B. (1984). Survey of academic writing tasks. *Written Communication, 1,* 247–280.

Cameron, J., & Pierce, W. D. (1994). Reinforcement, reward, and intrinsic motivation: A meta-analysis. *Review of Educational Research, 64,* 363–423.

Chai, C. (2006). Writing plan quality: Relevance to writing scores. *Assessing Writing, 11,* 198–223.

Chanquoy, L. (2001). How to make it easier for children to revise their writing: A study of text revision from 3rd to 5th grades. *British Journal of Educational Psychology, 71,* 15–41.

Coker, D. (2006). Impact of first-grade factors on the growth and outcomes of urban schoolchildren's primary-grade writing. *Journal of Educational Psychology, 98,* 471–488.

Cordova, D. I., & Lepper, M. R. (1996). Intrinsic motivation and the process of learning: Beneficial effects of contextualization, personalization, and choice. *Journal of Educational Psychology, 88,* 715–730.

Fisher, B. (1991). Getting started with writing. *Teaching K–8,* 49–51.

Gottfried, A. E., Fleming, J. S., & Gottfried, A. W. (2001). Continuity of academic intrinsic motivation from childhood through late adolescence: A longitudinal study. *Journal of Educational Psychology, 93,* 3–13.

Gradwohl, J., & Schumacher, G. (1989). The relationship between content knowledge and topic choice in writing. *Written Communication, 6,* 181–195.

Graham, S. (2006). Strategy instruction and the teaching of writing: A meta-analysis. In C. A. MacArthur, S. Graham, & J. Fitzgerald (Eds.), *Handbook of writing research* (pp. 187–207). New York: Guilford.

Graham, S., Berninger, V., Abbott, R., Abbott, S., & Whitaker, D. (1997). Role of mechanics in composing of elementary school students: A new methodological approach. *Journal of Educational Psychology, 89,* 170–182.

Graham, S., Harris, K., & Fink, B. (2000). Is handwriting causally related to learning to write? Treatment of handwriting problems in beginning writers. *Journal of Educational Psychology, 92,* 620–633.

Graham, S., & Perin, D. (2007a). A meta-analysis of writing instruction for adolescent students. *Journal of Educational Psychology, 99*, 445–476.

Graham, S., & Perin, D. (2007b). *Writing next: Effective strategies to improve writing of adolescents in middle and high schools—A report to Carnegie Corporation of New York.* Washington, DC: Alliance for Excellent Education.

Harris, K., & Graham, S. (1996). *Making the writing process work: Strategies for composition and self-regulation* (2nd ed.). Cambridge, MA: Brookline Books.

Harris, K. R., & Graham, S. (1999). Programmatic intervention research: Illustrations from the evolution of self-regulated strategy development. *Learning Disability Quarterly, 22*, 251–262.

Hayes, J. (2004). What triggers revision? In L. Allal, L. Chanquoy, & P. Largy (Eds.), *Revision: Cognitive and instructional processes* (pp. 9–20). Boston: Kluwer.

Hillocks, G., Jr. (1986). *Research on written composition: New directions for teaching.* Urbana, IL: National Conference on Research in English/ERIC Clearinghouse on Reading and Communication Skills.

Hillocks, G., Jr. (2002). *The testing trap: How state writing assessments control learning.* New York: Teachers College Press.

Hillocks, G., Jr., & Smith, M. W. (2003). Grammars and literacy learning. In J. Flood, D. Lapp, J. R. Squire, & J. M. Jensen (Eds.), *Handbook of research on teaching the English language arts* (2nd ed., pp. 721–737). Mahwah, NJ: Erlbaum.

Holliway, D. R., & McCutchen, D. (2004). Audience perspective in young writers' composing and revising. In L. Allal, L. Chanquoy, & P. Largy (Eds.), *Revision: Cognitive and instructional processes* (pp. 87–101). Boston: Kluwer.

Lepper, M. R., Corpus, J. H., & Iyengar, S. S. (2005). Intrinsic and extrinsic motivational orientations in the classroom: Age differences and academic correlates. *Journal of Educational Psychology, 97*, 184–196.

McCutchen, D. (1988). Functional automaticity in children's writing: A problem of metacognitive control. *Written Communication, 5*, 306–324.

Meichenbaum, D., & Biemiller, A. (1992). In search of student expertise in the classroom: A metacognitive analysis. In M. Pressley, K. Harris, & J. Guthrie (Eds.), *Promoting academic competence and literacy in school* (pp. 3–56). San Diego, CA: Academic Press.

National Commission on Writing. (2004, September). *Writing: A ticket to work . . . or a ticket out, A survey of business leaders.* Retrieved August 21, 2008, from www.writingcommission .org/report.html.

National Commission on Writing. (2005, July). *Writing: A powerful message from state government.* Retrieved August 21, 2008, from www .writingcommission.org/report.html.

Oka, E. R. (2005). Motivation. In S. W. Lee (Ed.), *Encyclopedia of school psychology* (pp. 330–335). Thousand Oaks, CA: Sage.

Pajares, F. (2003). Self-efficacy beliefs, motivation, and achievement in writing: A review of the literature. *Reading and Writing Quarterly, 19*, 139–158.

Pajares, F., Johnson, M. J., & Usher, E. L. (2007). Sources of writing self-efficacy beliefs of elementary, middle, and high school students. *Research in the Teaching of English, 42*, 104–120.

Pajares, F., & Valiante, G. (2006). Self-efficacy beliefs and motivation in writing development. In C. A. MacArthur, S. Graham, & J. Fitzgerald (Eds.), *Handbook of writing research* (pp. 158–170). New York: Guilford.

Pedulla, J., Abrams, L., Madaus, G., Russell, M., Ramos, M., & Miao, J. (2003). *Perceived effects of state-mandated testing programs on teaching and learning: Findings from a national survey of teachers.* Chestnut Hill, MA: National Board on Educational Testing and Public Policy, Boston College.

Pressley, M. (2002). What I have learned up until now about research methods in reading education. In D. L. Schallert, C. M. Fairbanks, J. Worthy, B. Maloch, & J. V. Hoffman (Eds.), *51st Yearbook of the National Reading Conference* (pp. 33–44). Oak Creek, WI: National Reading Conference.

Pritchard, R. J., & Honeycutt, R. L. (2006). The process approach to writing instruction: Examining its effectiveness. In C. A. MacArthur, S. Graham, & J. Fitzgerald (Eds.), *Handbook of writing research* (pp. 275–290). New York: Guilford.

Rog, L. J. (2007). *Marvelous minilessons for teaching beginning writing, K–3*. Newark, DE: International Reading Association.

Sadoski, M., Willson, V., & Norton, D. (1997). The relative contributions of research-based composition activities to writing improvement in the lower and middle grades. *Research in the Teaching of English, 31,* 120–150.

Scardamalia, M., & Bereiter, C. (1986). Research on written composition. In M. Wittrock (Ed.), *Handbook of research on teaching* (3rd ed., pp. 778–803). New York: Macmillan.

Schunk, D. H. (2003). Self-efficacy for reading and writing: Influence of modeling, goal setting, and self-evaluation. *Reading and Writing Quarterly, 19,* 159–172.

Schunk, D. H., & Zimmerman, B. J. (1997). Developing self-efficacious readers and writers: The role of social and self-regulatory processes. In J. T. Guthrie & A. Wigfield (Eds.), *Reading engagement: Motivating readers* through *integrated instruction* (pp. 34–50). Newark, DE: International Reading Association.

Taylor, B. M., Pearson, P. D., Peterson, D. S., & Rodriguez, M. C. (2003). Reading growth in high-poverty classrooms: The influence of teacher practices that encourage cognitive engagement in literacy learning. *Elementary School Journal, 104,* 3–28.

Turner, J. (1993). Situated motivation in literacy instruction. *Reading Research Quarterly, 28,* 288–289.

Voss, V. V. (2001). The effect of writing process training for teachers on the Texas Assessment of Academic Skills reading and writing scores of students in grades 3–8 (Doctoral dissertation, Texas A&M University-Commerce, 2001). *Dissertation Abstracts International, 63*(01), 75A.

Walker, B. J. (2003). The cultivation of student self-efficacy in reading and writing. *Reading and Writing Quarterly, 19,* 173–187.

Zammuner, V. L. (1995). Individual and cooperative computer-writing and revising: Who gets the best results? *Learning and Instruction, 5,* 101–124.

Index